"Tim Reddish, trained both in physics and theology, has a nimble mind, and this probing of the relationship between human suffering and God is deft and profound. But mainly this is a deeply personal book, one in which Reddish's own experience with loss and grief sends him farther along the path of faith. His journey takes him not to neatly crafted answers but instead to the cross of Jesus Christ. Readers of this book will learn much, and they will also be powerfully moved."

—Thomas G. Long
author of *What Shall We Say? Evil, Suffering, and the Crisis of Faith*

"Drawing from Scripture, tradition, science, and his own very personal experience with tragedy, Tim Reddish offers readers a clear, comprehensive, and compelling response to the problem of evil—one that doesn't require us to accept that the horrendous suffering people often endure is part of God's grand plan but that nevertheless offers people great hope and comfort. Whether or not readers end up agreeing with every aspect of Reddish's proposal—I do not—they will find a wealth of helpful insights in this powerful book."

—Gregory A. Boyd
author of *Is God to Blame?* and *Satan and the Problem of Evil*

"Lucid, thought-provoking, insightful, and deeply personal. Reddish shows how the path of suffering can be transformative, even enabling intimacy with our Trinitarian God, who participates in our suffering and with that of all creation. The Trinity's journey of suffering love to the cross can become more profoundly real through our own experiences of pain and brokenness."

—Richard Rohr
author of *The Divine Dance* and *Job and the Mystery of Suffering*

"Rooted in his own experience of life's limits, Tim Reddish has written a thoughtful account of the problem of human suffering and the Christian response to it. This book is well-informed by some of the best treatments of the subject in contemporary literature. It is written in a clear and readable manner, and should serve Christian and non-Christian discussion groups admirably."

—Douglas John Hall
author of *God and Human Suffering* and *The Cross in Our Context*

"Once we set aside belief in a controlling God, faith in God becomes more interesting, not less so. Reddish explores the implications in this readable and provocative book. The results create a new vision of God and a way to make sense of suffering and joy."

—Thomas Jay Oord
author of *The Uncontrolling Love of God*

"A wise, illuminating, and moving book in practical theology—a real pleasure to read."

—Keith Ward
author of *Divine Action* and *Christ and the Cosmos*

"In this little gem of a book, Reddish brings the full weight of his rigorous scientific and theological mind to bear on questions of suffering and God in this world. Grounded in his experience of grief, having suffered the untimely death of his beloved wife, Anne, Reddish examines central doctrines of the faith to consider how they speak into the lives of real people living and dying in the here and now. He examines biblical sources, historical and contemporary theology, and especially the theology of the cross to explore questions of theodicy for Christians in today's world. It is an engaging and thoughtful read, written from the heart of a lively and invigorated faith."

—Pamela R. McCarroll
author of *Waiting at the Foot of the Cross*

Does God Always Get What God Wants?

Brian McLaren

Does God Always Get What God Wants?

An Exploration of God's Activity in a Suffering World

TIM REDDISH

CASCADE *Books* · Eugene, Oregon

DOES GOD ALWAYS GET WHAT GOD WANTS?
An Exploration of God's Activity in a Suffering World

Cascade Books
An Imprint of Wipf and Stock Publishers
199 W. 8th Ave., Suite 3
Eugene, OR 97401

www.wipfandstock.com

PAPERBACK ISBN: 978-1-5326-1764-5
HARDCOVER ISBN: 978-1-4982-4248-6
EBOOK ISBN: 978-1-4982-4247-9

Cataloguing-in-Publication data:

Names: Reddish, Tim.

Title: Does God always get what God wants? : an exploration of God's activity in a suffering world / Tim Reddish.

Description: Eugene, OR : Cascade Books, 2018 | Includes bibliographical references.

Identifiers: ISBN 978-1-5326-1764-5 (paperback) | ISBN 978-1-4982-4248-6 (hardcover) | ISBN 978-1-4982-4247-9 (ebook)

Subjects: LCSH: Theodicy. | Suffering—Religious aspects—Christianity. | Good and evil—Religious aspects—Christianity.

Classification: BT160 .R43 2018 (paperback) | BT160 .R43 (ebook)

Manufactured in the U.S.A.   03/14/18

Front cover: stained glass window of *The Trinity* from Trinity Lutheran Church, Moorhead, Minnesota (http://www.trinitymhd.org), created by David Hetland. Used with permission.

All scriptural references are from either the NRSV or the NIV Bible translations.

In chapter 9, the excerpt of Anne's funeral meditation by Rev. Mary Templer is used with permission.

For Philip

In loving memory of Anne Carolyn Reddish, neé Camotta
(1961–2011)

O that my words were recorded!
That they were written on a scroll,
That they were inscribed with an iron tool on lead,
Or engraved on a rock forever!
I know that my Redeemer lives,
And that in the end he will stand upon the earth;
And after my skin has been destroyed,
Yet in my flesh I will see God.
I myself will see him with my own eyes—I, and not another.
How my heart yearns within me!

—JOB 19:23–27

Contents

Acknowledgments

About ten years ago I was browsing in a Borders bookstore when I noticed a book on suffering by Gregory Boyd entitled *Is God to Blame?* I bought it; with a catchy title like that, how could I not! I later devoured it. Its contents caused me to read other theological books by authors with similar views, such as: John Sanders, William Hasker, and Clark Pinnock. I was already reflecting deeply on my own understanding of God's providence in response to my experience of suffering, and so Boyd's book was perfect timing in helping me reformulate my own thinking and in articulating my views. So, I'd like to thank those authors and *many* others who have helped shape my thinking over the years—as evidenced within this book. Special mention is also due to N. T. Wright; your pastoral and academic books have influenced and encouraged me greatly, and continue to do so: thank you.

I would like to take this opportunity to express my heartfelt thanks to all the physicians, nurses, and staff of the Windsor Regional Cancer Center and Windsor Regional Hospital for all your attentiveness and diligence in your care for Anne. I would especially like to mention: Dr. J. Mathews (medical oncologist), Dr. R. K. Parashar (surgeon), Dr. A. Shamisa (neurosurgeon), Dr. K. Schneider (radiation oncologist), Dr. C. Leighton and Ms. R. DiBiase (palliative care), Ms. D. Fawdry (clinical trials liaison), and Dr. J. F. Shaw (family doctor). Without your effort and skill, Anne would not have had the quality of life that she had following her first diagnosis of breast cancer. I especially thank Drs. Mathews and Leighton, and Ms. Fawdry for your outstanding care that was well above the call of duty. Our frequent trips to the Cancer Center quickly became visits to a *haven of hope*, rather than to a place one dreads.

I wish to acknowledge University Community Church for your support to Anne, Philip, and myself, both during Anne's illness and following her death. I especially acknowledge my dear friends Mary Templer (UCC's former minister) and her husband, Andrew. Thank you for walking with us day-by-day on our journey. I also thank Frank and Ruth, and other members of our book study group, and our many UCC friends. Without your friendship and care, we would have been overwhelmed by our experience of suffering. Thank you for your steadfastness over those years. Furthermore, the Templer's demonstrated exceptional care for a widower by effectively adopting me into their family for over a year. Looking back, it was a remarkable period of time and it modeled the body of Christ in action for our church. Andrew and Mary: Thank you for your generosity, friendship, and encouragement.

Of course there are many others to acknowledge and thank, such as the group affectionately known as the "English Ladies," my Physics Department colleagues, and my then employer—the University of Windsor—for all your patience, care, and support for Anne and me. In addition to my parents and wider family members, there are long-standing friends in Britain (from Manchester and Newcastle) and elsewhere, such as Pete and Jen, Russ and Ann, Peter and Linda, Maria and Alan, and Lilian, who have each demonstrated kindness and support in various ways. Thank you.

For all those who *prayed* for us—thank you!

Philip: neither of us would have chosen for ourselves this road to travel down. But we continue to walk it together, and alongside those we love. I love you and I am proud of you—and I know your mom would be too. Greer: you are an amazing daughter-in-law! I acknowledge all your care and support during those difficult years, especially given you were then only just getting to know the Reddish family. Anne knew with deep sadness that she would miss the delightful experience of being a grandmother. Consequently, to my grandchildren, Arthur and Beatrice: know that you would have been dearly loved by Anne.

Speaking of Anne, she would have been astonished to think that part of her story would end up being disseminated in this fashion. At Dr. Leighton's request, she once bravely told of her experiences as a cancer patient to medical students at the University of Windsor. In light of her willingness to tell of her journey publicly, and for other reasons, I am confident she would be delighted with the contents of this book and would wish it to impact positively the lives of others.

Although we all experience tragedy and grief, our lives do eventually move on. For me that included a major transition from physics to theology as I became a seminary student at Knox College, at the University of Toronto. I express my thanks to my professors and fellow students for participating in that remarkable and enriching experience. I want to especially acknowledge my wife, Mary, for the joy and happiness we share on this exciting new journey together—along with Adam, Andrew, Jonathan, and Julia. Thank you too for your patience in reading this manuscript and in making many excellent suggestions to improve the text. I love you!

Finally, I want to thank all at Cascade Books, especially Matthew Wimer, Brian Palmer, and my editor, Charlie Collier. Thank you for believing in this project.

Introduction

The question "How can a loving and powerful God allow suffering?" is one of the most formidable obstacles to faith in God that the postmodern generation faces. Many are unwilling to open themselves to any other dimensions of Christianity unless Christians are prepared to engage in a serious and honest discussion on this issue. And there are Christians who have abandoned their faith because personal tragedy has destroyed their understanding of God or their assumptions concerning God's activity in the world. The issue of linking the God of love with the existence of suffering and evil is one that will not go away. Everyone has a view on this topic—professionals, such as philosophers, theologians, chaplains, pastors, and medical practitioners, as well as the everyday person. These views are tested in the fire of suffering, and some of them evaporate in smoke, leaving people in a state of crisis and confusion. Yet we need a response to this question—even if it is only a tentative one—if we are to have some kind of meaning to our existence and so live grounded with a strong sense of hope and purpose.

Whatever worldview we have provides us with some sort of answer to the perennial issue of suffering. A worldview of merit leaves us with something of substance—not just ash—in the bottom of the crucible, once the fire has cooled. If that residue is precious, we can treasure it and build upon it for the future. After all, being left with stony bitterness is counterproductive to wholesome living. Too often our experiences leave us with more questions than answers and we are left in a state of meaninglessness. What are we to do?

During the raging fires of suffering is *not* the time to explore such questions. But once the initial pain subsides, it is wise to reflect and examine the remains in the crucible. An intense experience of personal suffering can help us rewrite our *embedded* theology—our *assumed* understanding of both God and divine action. Indeed, theology is informed by Scripture, reason, tradition, and experience; all four aspects are important. Although the relative proportions vary in different Christian traditions, Scripture is foundational. At the end of the day, however, a theology that is not also grounded in reality, our *experience*, will not be taken seriously—either by ourselves or by others.

This book arises from experience. In January 2011, my first wife, Anne, died of breast cancer at the age of forty-nine. We had been married for twenty-eight years. Any wisdom within these pages has emerged because of Anne's story and our six-year journey down the road of living with cancer. These insights were therefore gained while traveling along a painful and unwanted path, and from questions raised by friends and fellow Christians.

Our experience of suffering challenges the *kind of God* we believe in, along with questions about the *kind of world* God has created—and the *relationship between the two*. All three are addressed in this book. For many, the first is obvious: God is the all-powerful, all-knowing God of perfect love. Many regard God as the one who is in ultimate control of everything. We imagine God as having a supreme voice-activated console that runs the world; God speaks and it comes to pass. After all, in Genesis 1 we read that the world was created and ordered by God's almighty command! If that is the case, and if God is good as Christians maintain, then *why* is there evil in the world? And so much of it? If we are honest, suffering causes us to doubt or question that traditional understanding of the Divine. If God is omnipotent, why doesn't God do *more* to alleviate pain and suffering in the world? Or more personally, why didn't God heal Anne? Did our prayers make any difference? How do we make sense of these issues? Can we make sense of them? Should we even try? These kinds of questions are explored in this book. It's OK to ask hard questions. It's OK to express our doubts, and even our anger. Remember, there is no such thing as faith without doubt—both are an integral part of our lives. If there were no possibility of doubt, we wouldn't need faith![1]

In our comfortable Western society, we have a tendency to think that we are "in control" of our lives and our futures. We plan, we set goals, we have expectations, and we work hard to achieve our objectives. But then life events happen: accidents, serious illness, divorce, job loss, cancer, and—much worse—terrible tragedies like the Sandy Hook Elementary School mass shooting in Connecticut, and our dreams and aspirations are

1. See Newbigin, *Proper Confidence*, 24–25.

shattered.[2] It is then that we suddenly realize we are not as in control of our lives as we imagine ourselves to be. One of the sobering things about pain and suffering is that we are confronted with our own mortality, and we are forced to recognize how small we are in the grand scheme of things. For many, such times make us think more about God.

The Christian tradition emphasizes that God has revealed himself to humankind—ultimately in the person of Jesus, the *very* image of God (Col 1:15). That's pretty *amazing* if you think about it; but it is so easy to distort that picture. For example, some people subconsciously view the relationship between Jesus and God the Father to be a bit like a good cop, bad cop duo. The human Jesus they can relate to, but God is perceived to be stern and unapproachable—yet the one with real power. We pray to Jesus as if he is the one who can *persuade* God the Father to come to our aid and to be on our side. There is doubt as to whether Jesus and God the Father are truly team players having the same end in mind. While we may know in our *heads* this misrepresentation is not the case, our *hearts'* response reveals what we truly believe. In the middle of a crisis, we tend to resort to our hearts' perception of God, i.e., to our unreflective, embedded theology. And that our view of the Divine may collapse under the burden of suffering. What *kind of God* we believe in is vitally important. God's character matters.

While Christian creeds affirm a Trinitarian God, we too often fragment the Father, Son, and Spirit—as mentioned above. For some, the Spirit is not personal, but merely an ethereal positive influence or life-force, and Jesus was simply an inspirational moral teacher. What remains then is "God," the Creator—or a Higher Being. But such a deity, though powerful, can all too easily be perceived to be disinterested and distant. This kind of God is not very inspiring, especially in a crisis.

There are other Christians who faithfully attend church each week and give 10 percent of their income to "God's work." That is an honorable sign of their strong commitment. Yet for some of these Christians, this loyalty is really an expression of their subliminal personal covenant with God. They go to church and give their money and in return they expect an all-powerful God to protect them and their loved ones. This seems to function well until life events happen. Then they wonder what went wrong on God's side of this divine protection racket. Like the righteous Job, God

2. Like the Dunblane massacre in 1996, Sandy Hook was particularly heinous as young school children were deliberately targeted by the killer. Of course, this does not belittle the horrors of other more recent senseless tragedies, like those in Las Vegas and Orlando.

has let them down and there is disappointment with God.[3] Evidently, it is not just the kind of God we believe in that is important, but *God's activity* within creation.

This book is divided into three parts. Like a healthy sandwich, the first and last chapters are the bread made with the gritty whole grains of real life. The other chapters are the meat, together with a mixture of other fresh ingredients and spiced with condiments. There is an intermingling of theology, church history, philosophy, science, and biblical studies; an accessible combination providing a synthesis to chew on. Since life is complex, we must expect diverse ingredients to contribute to this exploration of God's activity in a suffering world. I wholeheartedly believe this sandwich is tasty and satisfying. It contains a good news message that gives hope and leads to wholeness as we discover what God has done—and is doing—about evil.

The first short chapter introduces you to Anne's story. It is a reminder—not that we ever really need one—that pain and suffering are *real*. Dreams are shattered; families, friendships, and our social circles are impacted indelibly. Those whose lives have been touched by cancer will vividly recall that this involves waiting for medical tests . . . and their results, followed by surgery, then chemotherapy, radiotherapy . . . and more tests. All this tests our patience and perseverance. And our faith, too.

Living with cancer for six years caused me to read, reflect, and process. What I believed at the time of Anne's death is summarized at the end of chapter 1 and is the first nibble of the meaty part of the sandwich. Briefly, I came to the conclusion that pain and suffering are *outside* of God's desires for our lives, rather than something God *specifically planned* or *sent* as a test of faith or as a means to refine character. Consequently, God was *not* to blame for Anne's cancer. This seems so obvious with hindsight, yet I don't recall ever hearing a sermon on this kind of thinking. So I did more reading and discovered many theologians agreed: *God does not always get what God wants*. Some might find this conclusion surprising, shocking, even radically disturbing, because they believe God is "in control." Yet this insight liberates us to partner with God in opposing suffering, rather than fighting against a sovereign God.

But what do we mean by "sovereignty," and how does that relate with our understanding of God's power? This matter, along with the character and

---

3. This can be compounded if a Christian believes that God has clearly "guided" them in making a major decision. And then when life events happen, one is left wondering how this enforced detour fits in with God's "plan." (*Disappointment with God* is also the title of a well-known book by best-selling author Philip Yancey.)

nature of God, will be explored briefly in chapter 2.[4] The metaphor of God as an almighty king has a long history, beginning during the monarchical period of the Old Testament. Much later, following Emperor Constantine, the ties between church and state in the West established Christendom. This reinforced the connection between God and a monarch or ruler, so infusing influence, power, and dominance into a Christian worldview. In such a cultural and religious setting it was relatively easy to believe in the classical attributes of God, namely: unchanging, invulnerable, all-powerful, and all-knowing. It was this "all-controlling" God that was deemed to be the Creator and Sustainer of the world. Despite the collapse of Christendom over the last century,[5] this traditional view of God—referred to as *classical theism*—is still very influential. It is preached every Sunday in our churches and is an integral part of theological discourse in our seminaries. Yet, as mentioned earlier, we claim to believe in a *Trinitarian* God. Chapter 2 reminds us of what that entails, as we tend to overlook this postbiblical doctrine that is fundamental to Christianity. Moreover, I believe a Trinitarian view of God is vitally important in our understanding of God and the problem of suffering.

The relationality within the Trinity is explored further in chapter 3, where we briefly consider the question: "Why did Jesus have to die?" As we will see, our traditional responses to that question tend to fragment the Trinity, driving a wedge between Jesus and God the Father. If we really believe that God did not *spare* his Son but *sent* him into the world to die, then that inevitably colors how we regard God when *we* experience pain and suffering. Are there alternative ways to view the cross? Yes! I believe we need to embrace what Luther termed "the crucified God" and view the

4. Incidentally, while traditionally God is often referred to as "he," it is widely acknowledged that God has *no* gender. Consequently, sentences are conventionally constructed to avoid the usage of a personal pronoun for God, or even to reference God as "Father," in formal, contemporary theology. (Referring to the Holy Spirit as "she" is the acceptable exception!) One downside of this, in addition to some tortuous sentence structures, is that it has the tendency to diminish God as *person*. The *relational* Trinity and God as *person* are, however, key themes in this book. Therefore I will follow the traditional custom of using male pronouns here, and speaking of the Trinity as "Father, Son, and Spirit," but this usage should *not* be seen as endorsing patriarchy or as assigning to God a gender.

5. Douglas John Hall nevertheless reminds us that as Christians we believe: "God is at work in history, and that the divine Spirit creates, recreates, judges and renews the 'body of Christ.' What is happening in the churches of Europe and North America today cannot, therefore, be received by us as if it were devoid of purpose. The hand of God is in it!" Hall, *Christendom and Christianity*, 41.

view the cross as the ultimate expression of the relational Trinity's identification with a suffering creation. Of necessity, this is a *suffering* God, the antithesis of a deity that is invulnerable to—or uninterested in—creation.

The next two chapters consider various Christian responses to the problem of evil; chapters 4 and 5 focus on "natural" and "moral" evil, respectively—although there is necessarily some overlap. Natural evils include: earthquakes, tsunamis, droughts, and volcanoes, together with disease and death. Chapter 4 also addresses the pain and suffering—even cruelty—that we observe in the biological world, acknowledging that this existed long before humans arose on our planet. While Christians affirm God's creation is "very good" (Gen 1:31), it is evidently an *untamed* world. Chapter 5 considers the many evils that arise from the choices humans make, whether individually (e.g., abuse, murder, etc.) or collectively—even state-supported (e.g., slavery, torture, ethnic "cleansing," etc.). This chapter explores the question: "Does God always get what God wants?" Some Christians respond, "Emphatically, yes," others say, "Definitely not." We will explore various rationales, and since each can claim biblical support, further insights from theology, philosophy, and science can prove helpful. Each perspective has strengths and weaknesses; while I think some are much better than others, we can't help but acknowledge that suffering never makes perfect sense. But *where* we locate the mystery is helpful. We have three choices: (a) the mind of God, (b) God's complex creation, and (c) the relationship between the two—the mystery of divine action.[6] For those Christians who believe "God is in control," the location of the mystery can ultimately *only* be in the mind of God. But this, I suggest, is not only too simplistic, it is also dangerously misleading. . . .

Rational insights are important—for God gave us minds to use—and they can be faith enhancing. Nevertheless, our frustration at the existence and persistence of suffering brings us to the key question: *What is God doing about evil?* This is explored in chapter 6 by considering the overall biblical narrative. The Bible should not be seen as simply a depository of promises to "claim" in tough times, rather its authors are telling stories of God's activity in the world. What, then, is God doing about evil, pain, and suffering? Many Christians are familiar, perhaps overly so, with well-known Bible stories and Israel's history. But if God inspired the authors, are there repetitive themes that—taken together—reinforce each other and

6. Depending on one's theology, these three options are not necessarily mutually exclusive.

so provide a bigger picture of God's activity within history? I believe so; in which case, the biblical record is not just about Israel, but *the story we find ourselves in*. A narrative in which we can not only recognize and experience God's presence—critically important though that undoubtedly is—but also one that brings genuine hope in suffering and purpose to our lives. The plotline inevitably passes through the data point of Jesus the Messiah, the person who defies all categorization—eventually resulting in the doctrine of the Trinity. And so we return briefly to the cross, and there we discover afresh what the Trinitarian God did—and is doing—about evil.

The mystery of divine action is explored further in chapters 7 and 8 where we consider miracles and prayer, respectively. Is praying for a miracle a bit like a quarterback's last ditch "hail Mary" pass in American football? (And even there, there has to be a receiver suitably placed and able to catch the ball!) Is there a more positive way of thinking about miracles? Chapter 7 presents a preliminary theology of miracles as *glimpses of the future in the present*. It also considers some of the troubling questions we have concerning miracles, such as why we don't experience more of them today. Chapter 8 explores aspects of Romans 8, focusing on Paul's remarkable claim that the Christian's prayer is *co-prayer with Spirit*—we *never* pray alone. Knowing that God *always* hears our prayers, and that they make a *real* difference in the world, is a powerful message of encouragement, especially in times of suffering.

Chapter 9 returns to Anne's story, the complementary part of the sandwich to chapter 1. Written months after Anne died, it relates Anne's death and her funeral, and meditates on dying, waiting, and the foundational Christian hope of the resurrection—which we celebrated on the first Easter after Anne died. Suffering is *never* the last word.

I invite you to share in this human story of Anne and thereby find encouragement and hope—and witness God powerfully at work. But more than that, let us wrestle with these complex issues together. In so doing, we must be willing to have our own theological worldview challenged. The intent here is not to simply rail against God—although a theology of protest is a valid response—but to explore and develop what I consider to be the refined gold in the bottom of the crucible. The goal is to nurture faith and to better understand God and God's activity in the world. But this cannot be merely a matter of head knowledge, we also need to acclimatize ourselves to the Spirit's presence and so experience the suffering God with us on our journey.

Finally, let us remember that as Christians we are empowered by the Holy Spirit and called to be God's agents of justice, restoration, and hope. So let us therefore move forward together and partner with our Trinitarian God to counter all the effects of evil in this needy world, and to help further God's reign.

1

Crisis and *Credo*

The way they bore their suffering was a genuine inner achievement. It is this spiritual freedom—which cannot be taken away—that makes life meaningful and purposeful.

—VIKTOR FRANKL

Crisis

The telephone rang in my office and, moments later, my cell phone was ringing. I later found out that our home phone was being called too. It was our oncologist calling us with details of an urgent consultation with a neurosurgeon: he was expecting to see us in the Emergency Room of Hotel Dieu Hospital. I met Anne and our minister and close friend, Mary, in the waiting area of the hospital. I knew that Anne's neck was causing her intense pain, and I realized that our situation must be critical to warrant such immediate attention. Anne had undergone a bone scan the day before and we were due to fly to England in two days' time; it now looked like this trip would need to be canceled—as we had suspected. After a short while a triage nurse saw Anne's discomfort and brought her a neck brace. It provided instant relief that was visible on Anne's face. We soon got to see the specialist who gave us the bad news: "Your C2 vertebra in your neck is disintegrating with bone cancer and we have to stabilize your spine quickly. Any jarring or falling could cause acute damage, paralysis, or worse—so don't do anything until we can perform surgery." While we suspected a serious problem, as Anne's neck pain had been persistent, we were still stunned to hear the news. It meant that Anne's breast cancer had spread—and perhaps had spread to other areas, too.

Very early on Sunday morning Andrew, Mary's husband, and I sat together in an empty surgical waiting room. We had prayed, our church had prayed, and prayers were being offered by family and friends throughout the world. Eventually, a tired-looking neurosurgeon emerged to tell us the outcome. He had managed to fuse C1–C4. The C2 vertebra was severely damaged, especially on one side, and while the surgery had been very tricky, he was quietly optimistic of a good outcome.

Anne's road to recovery from this operation was long and painful. She described herself being "locked within her pain-filled body—a prisoner to pain." At one point early on she said, "If this level of pain is all I can now expect in life, then I would rather be dead." This was to be one of her darkest days.

Anne lived a full, active, and cheerful life for over five more years.

Anne and I kept most of the medical details private, except for our closest family and friends. While this may have fueled gossip, we were not trying to be overly secretive. This was just our attempt to protect Anne's dignity. Anyone with insight into breast cancer, or with access to the internet, knows the usual places to which breast cancer can metastasize, such as bone, liver, lungs, and brain. The need for being discreet had passed.

Anne's breast cancer was diagnosed in late 2004, two years before her neck surgery. We were told the cancer was virulent, so they therefore wanted to treat it aggressively. Anne was energized for that; she was determined to live! After surgery, she underwent chemotherapy followed by radiation, long-term medication, and periodic scans of various kinds.

In addition to the cancer metastasizing in her vertebrae, requiring surgery, radiation, intensive pain management and bone-strengthening drugs, the disease later spread to her liver, requiring further chemotherapy, and reoccurred in her breast, requiring a mastectomy and more radiation.

Early in 2009 Anne began to experience regular headaches that tended to occur in one region of her head. So we decided that we had better get that checked out along with a routine CT scan of her neck. The radiation oncologist told us the sad news that multiple brain tumors had been clearly identified. He then went on to sensitively explain the treatment plan. Of course we were devastated to hear of this development, especially as the brain is one region where standard chemotherapies cannot reach. Not long after we returned home, I pulled out the old *Ancient and Modern Hymnal* from my bookshelf and found "Love Divine, All Loves Excelling," the well-known Charles Wesley hymn that we had sung at our wedding. I was crying as I read out loud the last verse to Anne:

> Finish then Thy new creation:
> Pure and spotless let us be;
> Let us see Thy great salvation,
> Perfectly restored in Thee,
> Changed from glory into glory,
> Till in heaven we take our place,
> Till we cast our crowns before Thee,
> Lost in wonder, love and praise.

As we cried in each other's arms, I told Anne that heaven was now a step closer for her than it had been before. Later we received some encouraging news, namely, that the radiation treatment had reduced the size of the tumors.

Listed like this it seems like we never left the hospital! Indeed our lives revolved around hospital visits, tests, and a strict medication routine. Nevertheless we did have a life; but part of living with cancer for six years is addressing things such as stamina, lifestyle changes, being positive, enjoying small things, and appreciating what you have—rather than focusing on what you have lost, or what you fear you may lose.

During 2010 Anne and I were able to experience significant milestones together, including seeing our son, Philip, get married to Greer and seeing Philip graduate from university. Anne and I were able to fly to Vancouver and then drive through the Rockies together to Banff and Calgary. It was a wonderful six months. But then it became clear, to those who knew her well, that her memory was getting worse and she was struggling to find words at times. The brain tumors were back.

During the early years, when she first lost her hair from chemotherapy, Anne refused to wear a wig and wore distinctive head scarves under various colored baseball caps. She did not want people to look at her and instantly think "wig"! Later, when her hair grew back, she enjoyed short hair and her monthly visits to the hairdresser. In her last twenty months of life, after radiation to her head meant that her hair would not grow back, she decided to revisit the wig issue. We had some fun trying on different styles, laughing and joking at the outcome—it is always easy to know what does *not* work! Having quickly ascertained that a short-hairstyle wig was out of the question, Anne tried on a distinctive wig of just-above-the-shoulder-length hair with beautiful hues of red, brown, and a hint of gold. She loved it, exclaiming, "This is great because I look like my cousin." With this new bold look, Anne was instantly admired and while those who knew Anne realized it was a wig, most strangers did not. Once, while visiting a booth at Windsor's annual Art in the Park festival, a vendor exclaimed, "I love your hair color—*please* tell me the name of your hairdresser!" Believe me, that comment would make any female cancer patient feel good about herself.

The above description gives some small insight as to the kind of person Anne was and her determined approach to life while living with cancer. Seeing her function day by day you would never know of her resolute battle with the disease. She wanted to be seen as normal and live as full a life as possible, to the amazement and admiration of many.

Credo

In common with other academics and many thinking Christians, I suffer from the problem that my mind is insufficiently challenged or engaged by attendance of typical church services! I therefore supplement my worship by reading what many regard as in-depth theological books. Some of those books contain what traditional evangelicals might think of as radical thinking. I process these ideas, jettisoning some and embracing others, as I strive to know God better. Most of this happens in the privacy of my own mind, but the day eventually comes when these ideas spill out casually in conversation with others, as if they are quite normal. Ideas like: "I do not believe that it was part of God's plan for Anne to have cancer." Or, "I do not believe that God always gets God's own way."

One day, my supportive minister, Mary—out of concern as to how friends and congregants might react—challenged me to take the time to seriously think through whether or not I really believed these "new" ideas.[1] Or was I simply being provocative in order to stimulate lively discussion? "If you really believe these ideas are true," she continued, "then help us understand God and relate to God more meaningfully." It was a fair challenge

---

1. I have discovered these ideas are not particularly novel, but they are rarely articulated within most churches.

and request, particularly as my desire was—and is—to deepen faith, not to undermine it. So I took the time to write down a concise personal statement of belief, or *credo*. It was an intense and emotionally draining exercise to do, especially as this occurred only a matter of months following Anne's death. Here is what I wrote then; the rest of this book unpacks and develops these ideas.

I do not believe that God is the author of evil.

I do not believe that God *caused* Anne to have cancer.[2]

I do not believe that it was part of God's *plan* for Anne to have cancer, including any *secret* plan, or that somehow Anne's cancer and death was necessary—and beneficial—for the "greater good." (Incidentally, Anne did not believe that either. Rather, Anne strongly identified with a compassionate God, one who worked, walked, and suffered with us.)

A key question is simply, *Does God always get what God wants?* If the answer to that is yes, then clearly God is in meticulous control of the cosmos, and the fact that Anne got cancer is what God wanted and the fact that she died is also what God wanted.[3] If the answer to the question is no, does this automatically mean that God is weak? I think that is jumping to conclusions. It all depends on the nature of God's activity in the world; what God *can* and *cannot* do, not merely what God *wants* and does *not want* to do.

We end up thinking that if God is a micromanager, then the reason why Anne died young is located firmly in the mind of God. He is responsible. He was *capable* of healing her, but did not want to. We don't know why he is doing what he is doing in any given situation, we simply have to trust that he knows what he is doing! This "mystery" is often articulated as being part of God's unfathomable wisdom. Some people are happy to accept that "God is in control" and so find comfort. But when it comes to

2. You might ask, "Would any Christian say God *caused* Anne to die from cancer?" Strong Calvinists, for example, with their strict view of deterministic predestination, seem to have backed themselves into an uncomfortable corner on this issue. In order to avoid the troublesome word "caused," Roger Olson would rephrase the Calvinist's position to: "God *rendered certain* that Anne would die from cancer." It is an argument over semantics; it means the same thing! See Olson, *Against Calvinism*, 70–101. This will be discussed further in chapter 5.

3. This also raises the issue "What, then, is the point of praying?" and can lead to what can be thought of as Christian fatalism. This means, in effect, "what will be, will be," not because of some impersonal fate but because whatever God "wills" will inexorably happen. The issue of prayer will be explored in chapter 8.

close personal experience, like the death of a young wife and mother from cancer, a brutal murder of a child, a rape, and to larger scale things—such as wars and famines—then it is increasingly hard to maintain this acquiescence and simply close your eyes and trust God. If God is in absolute control and God's activity is a manifestation of his character, my response would not be to worship him, but to be afraid of him. Others will, understandably, get angry with such a God in the face of their suffering.

If, on the other hand, we see the character of God as imaged in Jesus Christ—as portrayed in the gospels—then God does not always get what God wants and we need to identify reasons, or at least establish a mental framework, however tentative and loosely bound, as to why this is the case.[4] For instance, that framework would include the shear complexity of the created order (to which God has endowed a strong degree of independence), and human free will. Certainly, much evil abounds because of our "sins of commission and omission"—both what we do and what we fail to do. So here we have two categories (human free will and the complexity of intermingling physical processes) that are "other" than God and in which we could locate the mystery of suffering.[5] This scenario, together with biblical evidence, can lead us to a different view of God's activity, one where God is continuing to establish his kingdom and where he invites us to become his partners. In this picture, God is totally good and not the author of evil, but it also implies that once God has given space for the freedom required for a world in which love and faith are genuinely possible, then God *cannot* revoke that decision without ruining the whole creation project. What we see now is that the world has somehow gone wrong—as it were. Nevertheless, God did not abandon the project. Instead God rolled up his sleeves, so to speak, and got involved in rescuing his creation. God does all that he can, within the constraints that he sovereignly setup at the beginning, to achieve his initial goal(s) and the end(s) he desires.

---

4. For example, I would argue that the death of John the Baptist was hardly something that God (or Jesus) *wanted* to happen (see Matt 14:1–13).

5. Some authors, like Gregory Boyd, would add a third possibility, namely, the free will of other created agents, such as angels and demons. This dualistic worldview is not uncommon in those Christian traditions that emphasize spiritual warfare with the "principalities and powers." Such a perspective is also a key feature of Gustaf Aulén's *Christus Victor* atonement metaphor/model, discussed in chapter 3. I am not eager to invoke spiritual warfare with physical consequences, but no one can rule out this possibility. This will be explored further in chapters 3–5.

Consequently, I believe that God does not always get his own way. I believe the present state of the world is not how God intended or wants it to be.

I believe God is love, good, all-wise, omnicompetent, and resourceful without limit.

I believe God knows all that is knowable.

I believe God desires a genuine give-and-take relationship with us; he responds and has compassion. God is vulnerable because love entails vulnerability.

I believe the creation project that God has embarked upon is not risk-free for God, because he sovereignly chose it to be that way. Yet God is not reckless, but he is prepared to take risks for the sake of love.

I believe God is not unchanging (immutable) or unfeeling (impassive). This is evident throughout Scripture and is most graphically demonstrated in the incarnation. If "the Word *became* flesh" (John 1:14), then God is not immutable. If "God so *loved* the world that he gave his son" (John 3:16), he is not impassive but is relational.

I believe that God, before the cosmos began, was literally omnipotent—as traditionally understood and proclaimed. But he did not want to use that power to coerce living beings with genuine free will to love him. Therefore, in sovereignly and freely choosing to create *this* kind of world, God willingly let go of certain aspects of his power. This self-limitation means that, if God is to remain consistent to his character and true to his purposes, there are certain things he cannot do, even if he wants to. This does not make God weak; rather his faithfulness to his character and purposes makes him trustworthy. God still has enormous power, but prefers to work by inspiration and persuasion—and through us—rather than by brute force.

I believe that God did all that was possible for him to do for Anne. I believe that our prayers, including our attitude to ask of God, rather than demand from him, helped God to achieve all that he could do in an open world and in our given situation. Prayer was not a waste of time. God responded. Naturally, we initially asked for complete healing. However, once the cancer had spread, it became clear that any healing would either be even more dramatic, or it was somehow not possible for Anne. That last clause is problematic for some because they assume an almighty God of absolute control. However, the way I see it is that it was "not possible" *not* because that was what God *wanted* for Anne, but because of the kind of creation God made. In other words, this situation was *not* deliberately planned by God, nor a manifestation of God's character. Rather, it is encapsulated in the complex framework that addresses why God does not always get what God wants. I am not overly concerned with precisely locating the root cause of Anne's specific cancer, i.e., pursuing the question: *Why?* I do not believe Anne's untimely death was due to lack of faith or prayer. It could have been simply due to the vast complexity of Anne's specific cancer and her particular body make-up.

I believe that God answered our prayers for peace and protection. We also prayed continually that God would multiply the effectiveness of the chemo- and radiotherapies Anne was receiving, and for God to microscopically target those treatments to the cancerous cells. We prayed for the "maximum benefits with the minimum of side effects." I believe God answered those prayers and this enabled Anne to live at least one more year with a very good quality of life. I believe that God actualized that possibility.

Once complete healing was evidently not going to happen, I began praying that her dying would be full of mercy and grace. I believed that this was still a real possible outcome and, looking back, I believe that God actualized that possibility too. Anne had no seizures and the aroma of God's love was evident in the hospital room in her last days.

I believe that God was continually by our side, walking with us. We were not abandoned by him. His Spirit was with us, and still continues to be a daily reality. Our family, friends, and church were also with us. No one (I hope!) interpreted Anne's cancer as a sign of God's judgment or displeasure and hence shunned us.

I believe that God is *not* the author of evil; rather, God *actively* works to bring good out of evil.

2

The Trinitarian God

If the mystery of the Trinity is the template of all reality, what we have in the Trinitarian God is the perfect balance between union and differentiation, autonomy and mutuality, identity and community.

—RICHARD ROHR

Introduction

What is God like? And how would we know? For the Christian, the starting point is that God is the "God of the Bible." But stating that is the beginning—not the end—of the matter. The God of the Bible is not simply to be equated with the God *portrayed* in the Bible. If we did, we might find the God described there to be fear-inducing, since God is depicted as a violent warrior or an almighty king in many places in the Old Testament. God is also described as a lawgiver and a righteous judge, as well as more comforting metaphors of a rock, a potter, a shepherd, a gardener, and a loving parent. Scripture contains a complex, even confusing, array of images for God. Nevertheless, Christians agree that God is not derived from studies of nature or philosophy but based on the biblical authors' understanding of God and God's actions in history. That understanding *evolved*—and continues to evolve. It was a journey of discovery,

9

first by the patriarchs (Abraham, Isaac, and Jacob) and their families, then by key leaders (such as Moses, Joshua, and Samuel), and later kings (like David and Solomon) and prophets (like Isaiah, Jeremiah, and Ezekiel). The Old Testament authors were, among other things, describing *their* understanding of what God is like and how God relates to the world.[1] Moreover, it is fair to assume that they were *not* writing with the whole history of humanity in mind, but to their own specific audiences and contexts. Israel's basic understanding of their God was in terms of a covenant, a binding promise of mutual relationship and commitment. God was *relational*, not an abstract, distant Divine but the personal "God of Abraham, Isaac and Jacob." For the Christian, God's supreme self-revelation to humankind was in the birth, life, death, resurrection, and ascension of Jesus, the Messiah, followed by the coming of the Spirit. I will call this complete package the *Christ-event*. Christians therefore rightly say: "If you want to know what God is like, look at Jesus." Nevertheless, the response to the original question "What is God like?" is still more complicated.

Christians often forget that in light of the Christ-event, the early church had to formulate a response to the question *"Who is Jesus?"* To a Jew, claiming Jesus was divine would be tantamount to blasphemy for: The LORD our God is *one* (see Deut 6:4). Theologians agree that the Bible does not present a clear doctrine of the Trinity. This doctrine—as we will see—arose later during the first few centuries CE. Christology wrestles with the "Who is Jesus?" question and orthodoxy affirms Jesus is more than the long-awaited Messiah; he is the incarnate Son of God. The God of the Bible does not, then, merely float off the pages of Scripture; the doctrine of God arises from deliberate theological reflection. Theology continually systematizes that doctrine by the use of reason, based on biblical insights, and informed by the broad, historical Christian tradition. All this is further shaped by our own contemporary context and experiences of God.

While church tradition affirms a *Trinitarian* God at its very core, Christians haven't always consistently thought of God in Trinitarian terms. Israel's God—YHWH, the Creator God—was readily syncretized with Plato's *demiurge* in the Hellenization of both Judaism *and* Christianity. This view of the Divine formed the basis of an imperial God with absolute qualities of immutability (unchangeable), impassivity (no negative emotions), omnipotence (all-powerful), omniscience (all-knowing), and eternality (timeless). These abstract attributes are still often assumed by Christians

---

1. See also Exod 34:6–7; Num 14:18; Neh 9:17; Joel 2:13; and Jonah 4:2.

today, with no second thought. This view of God is referred to as *classical theism*.

Much later in history—and with the development of a scientific worldview—the Creator God became merely the impersonal Designer and Instigator of the universe. This distant "god" of deism wound up the mechanism of a clockwork universe and then set it in motion along pre-determined lines. Around the same time, Jesus became an inspirational moral teacher and the mysterious Spirit was either forgotten or became a depersonalized life-force. While the church's creeds proclaimed the Trinity, in practice, Trinitarian thinking became a thin veneer on top of a Chris-tianized, platonic understanding of God.

Once this was recognized, notably by Karl Barth and Karl Rahner in the last century, a resurgence of Trinitarian thought began to occur. Never-theless, a philosophical view of the Divine continues to strongly influence theology and its rational discourse. For example—and perhaps not surpris-ingly—little is mentioned of the Trinity in the dialogue between science and Christianity.[2] And, as we shall see, the problem of evil and suffering is often posed in terms of the God of classical theism. Christians and critics alike tend to assume God is all-powerful, leading to certain expectations as to what a good God (Ps 136:1) *could* and *should* do about suffering. Because this is a common starting point to the problem of suffering, we will briefly consider what is meant by God's sovereignty and omnipotence. To place God's power in context, we need to first address the matter of divine pathos; can God be *affected* by creation? In chapters 4 and 5 we will consider vari-ous contemporary responses to the problem of evil, all of which have the deity of classical theism in mind. A Christian response, however, should be based primarily on *theological* reflection, not philosophical—although there is naturally overlap and dialogue between these disciplines. For that reason, the bulk of this chapter reminds us of our Trinitarian heritage. Since the doctrine of the Trinity is a postbiblical development, many Christians know little about how and why it arose. Many struggle to understand or articulate its significance or relevance. While it is so much easier to simply talk about "God," we lose something profound and important when we don't think and speak within a Trinitarian framework. This is especially true in the context of evil and suffering, as we will discover in later chapters. Traditional Christian responses to suffering, helpful though they can be,

2. Actually, current scholarship is now exploring this theme.

are severely misleading—even damaging—if they assume the God of classical theism.

Divine Pathos

Classical theism's God is deemed immutable, in other words, perfect, incorruptible, and unchanging. For God to change would either be for the worse, or imply that God was lacking in some quality—which cannot be. Therefore such a *static* God is best regarded as timelessly eternal, or *outside* of time. In addition, God is also understood to be impassive, i.e., unable to experience emotion, passion, suffering, or to be vulnerable to—or affected by—creation. (Such a stoic view of the Divine should be contrasted with the capricious nature of the gods of Greek mythology.) Now while immutability may seem consistent with a biblical understanding of God (e.g., Mal 3:6; Jas 1:17),[3] it is bewildering—given the biblical evidence—to see how impassivity could have been so readily absorbed within classical theism. For example, God is said to exhibit anger, jealousy, and wrath, as well as experience sadness, regret, and grief. It is too easy to dismiss all these words of emotion as anthropomorphisms or as divine accommodation, but if we do so, we pay the price of belittling the Judeo-Christian claim that God is a *person*.[4] The Bible claims that God's prime characteristic is *love* (1 John 4:8), and love implies a give-and-take relationship whereby the lover can be affected by the beloved. This not only results in the possibility of joy and compassion, but also in the potential for suffering and grief—as love can be rejected. To say that God can suffer implies that he is vulnerable and that what he desires can be obstructed. Some are troubled with the idea that a relational God can experience passion and voluntarily takes such risks for the sake of love. Instead they remain convinced that God is the unmoved Mover; such an aloof Divine is closer to that of deism than the Christian God. Most contemporary theologians reject the notion of divine impassivity, as do I, and—as we shall see—this opens wide the door to an

3. Daniel Migliore points out the key distinction: "What characterizes the depiction of God in the scriptural witness is *not* an abstract notion of changelessness but God's constancy and faithfulness to God's own nature and to God's covenant with the world." Migliore, *Faith Seeking Understanding*, 413, emphasis mine.

4. This is *not* to say that God as "person" is to be considered exactly like a human person; God experiences reality in a very different way from us, for God is not mortal. For example, the Trinitarian God does not experience loneliness or fear. See also Pinnock, *Most Moved Mover*, 88–92.

empathetic, compassionate God who responds to us and comes alongside us in the face of suffering.

God's Sovereignty and Power

What do we mean by omnipotent or "almighty," as the historical creeds describe God the Father? Fully aware of our own limitations, our instinctive response is to say: "God can do *anything*!" But is that really the case? Can God make a stone that is too heavy for him to lift? Can 2 + 2 = 5 for God? Can God draw square circles? Can God tell a lie? There is a serious point to such questions: they highlight that there are some things even "almighty" God cannot do. Instead, a philosopher might say that omnipotence means God can do anything that *for him* is *logically* possible, anything which does not involve a contradiction.[5] God is therefore subject to logic, just as we are, and cannot act in a way that is logically incoherent.

While many people have no issues with this, some Christians are deeply uncomfortable and perceive this as "limiting" God. The idea that God is subject to *anything* goes against their understanding of God's sovereignty. Instead, they would prefer to hold fast by faith to the words of the prophet: "'For my thoughts are not your thoughts, nor are your ways my ways,' says the LORD" (Isa 55:8). Theologians would be among the first to acknowledge the truth of that statement; no one is claiming to understand everything about God! Humans are, after all, finite beings. There will always be an element of mystery. But we must distinguish between mystery and nonsense. Christians must not proclaim gibberish and then assert we must accept it "by faith." It discredits Christianity to imply, as Huckleberry Finn put it, that "faith is believing what you know ain't so!" John Sanders observes,

> In my experience, virtually all those who claim God is above logic also say that God cannot be dishonest. People who say this are, in fact, affirming the rule of noncontradiction since they believe God cannot be both honest and dishonest. . . . [People can be] highly selective regarding when they play the "God is above logic" card.[6]

---

5. Based on Richard Swinburne's definition, as cited in Hasker, *Triumph of God over Evil*, 43–44. Anthony Thiselton, also citing Swinburne, insists, "God's sovereignty cannot facilitate acts that are *logically* self-contradictory." Thiselton, *Systematic Theology*, 54, his emphasis.

6. Sanders, *God Who Risks*, 34.

He concludes: "If our language about God is not subject to human logic, then we can say anything we want with impunity, and theological discourse will be pointless."[7] Intellectual and linguistic coherence is important if our understanding of God is to be meaningful, else our faith can become a belief in nonsense. God gave us rational minds and, presumably, expects us to use them!

The issue of logical consistency aside, many would still consider "almighty God" to mean that God can otherwise do anything he so desires. But I can't help but wonder if what we mean by "all-powerful" arises from the superhuman model of the Divine. We imagine God's power to be like that of a conquering monarch, only raised to the ultimate degree. Our Western culture is entranced by dominance, whether military, economic, or political, and we are enthralled by science and technology and the power *over* nature they have provided. At an individual level, we also claim our entitlement to personal freedoms and self-determinism, and we have convinced ourselves that we *can* control—and have the *right* to control—our destiny and well-being. We are captivated by the concept of power and of "being in control." But is our view of power and control, one that has been shaped by science and technology, the right approach to thinking about *God's* power? Or is this an example of a wish fulfillment, a projection of our own desires onto the divine nature?

William of Ockham (ca. 1285–1347) described God's power in two ways. The first is omnipotence in the absolute sense we instinctively assume. God had a free choice when he considered whether or not to create the universe. Moreover, when he was considering all the possible options and variations in the kind of creation he could make, God had absolute power to realize each of them—as long as they were logically coherent. Nothing *external* was (or is) being imposed on God, but once God sovereignly decided to make *this kind* of cosmos it meant that certain other options *for this cosmos* were no longer possible, even for God. For Ockham, God cannot *now* do everything because his previous decisions deliberately limit future possibilities.[8] In other words, God's actions limit God's

---

7. Ibid., 34. Anthony Thiselton adds, "Omnipotence . . . does not entail the ability to overcome *logical contradictions* (e.g., to make a round square) or *internal constraints* of character (e.g., to tell a lie or break a promise). Nothing would be gained by attributing to God the power to contradict logic, unless we regard God as creating an irrational universe." Thiselton, *Systematic Theology*, 75, his emphasis.

8. McGrath, *Christian Theology*, 210–11. He adds, "God's reliability and faithfulness is not externally constrained, but is determined by God's own character."

options—if God is to be consistent (or faithful) to his character. But it is important to recognize that divine self-limitation is freely *chosen* by God. God is sovereign over his sovereignty.

This notion of divine self-limitation has resurfaced in modern theology. Its biblical origin usually starts with Philippians 2:6–11; that ancient hymn/poem reads,

> [Christ Jesus] who, though he was in the form of God, did not regard equality with God as something to be exploited, but *emptied himself*, taking the form of a slave, being born in human likeness. And being found in human form, he *humbled himself* and became obedient to the point of death—even death on a cross.[9]

This passage speaks of Christ freely "emptying" (Gk. *kenosis*) himself to become human.[10] While it is easy to think that this only applies to Jesus, and therefore affects Christology and not the doctrine of God, yet—from a Trinitarian perspective—what we know about Christ informs our very understanding of God the Father and the Spirit. But why would God want to limit his power, you may ask? John Sanders gives helpful perspective: "Divine self-restraint should be understood as the *restraint of love* in concern for his creatures."[11] God does it for us, in the same way that a loving spouse chooses continually to be faithful to his/her partner throughout their marriage.

Sovereignty implies a monarch. No one is questioning God's *right* to be king; rather, we are exploring how God exercises his power. In considering what "almighty" God implies, it is helpful to regard God's sovereign power as an *enabling* power; a power *for*, rather than a power *over*—as in the sense of brute force.[12] Moreover, in the Genesis story we read that God *delegates* the sun and moon "to rule" the days and seasons (Gen 1:16). In modern language we might say our rotating planet's weather systems and seasons are governed by the sun and the laws of physics. Likewise, the command to "be fruitful and multiply" (Gen 1:22, 28) gives permission to creatures to *be* (and become) the "other" and further demonstrates God sharing his creative capabilities. God's blessing, in this context, is a word of empowerment.[13] Furthermore, God entrusts humankind to rule over the

9. Phil 2:6–8, emphasis mine.

10. See also Polkinghorne, *Work of Love*.

11. Sanders, *God Who Risks*, 241, emphasis mine.

12. Thiselton, *Systematic Theology*, 75.

13. Fretheim, *God and World*, 50.

fish, birds, and every living creature (Gen 1:28). We are God's representative agents on earth and divinely mandated to care responsibly for creation. God evidently is *not* a micromanager who meticulously controls every little detail in the cosmos. God is instead a power-sharing deity and gave creation a certain degree of autonomy. Sovereignty, then, is not synonymous with absolute power, but rather with the total freedom God has to use his power to accomplish God's creative and redemptive purposes in a manner consistent with God's character.[14]

Consequently, God does not see us as programmed robots, or puppets to be manipulated, or scripted actors on a stage. Instead, Christians maintain that God made us with genuine free will in order that we might enter into a relationship of love with him. Obviously this is *not* a relationship of equals—God is sovereign. The Creator is the Initiator (1 John 4:19). But it is nevertheless an authentic relationship as things happen by mutual consent. Moreover, God also wanted us to have the capability of having real faith, to trust each other, and to trust in him. Such faith can only take place if we are also truly free to doubt. Logically, if God made humankind with genuine free will then he cannot exercise total control over us. We must be free to *respond* to God's love, for that is the very nature of love. There is an element of risk here, but God evidently thinks it is worth taking. But, in doing so, God does not always get what God wants. Does this mean that God is weak? No, of course not!

This being the case, how should we understand "omnipotence"? Clark Pinnock writes,

> God's almightiness is not an abstract domineering power. It is essentially the *power of love*. A God who loves cannot be conceived in a deterministic way, like the power of the puppeteer. . . . God's power means that he is omnicompetent and can deal wisely with any circumstance that arises, not that he causes everything. It means that nothing can ultimately defeat him. . . . It takes omnipotence to create and manage freedom.[15]

Divine love qualifies divine power. Daniel Migliore states,

---

14. Migliore, *Faith Seeking Understanding*, 418. Clark Pinnock writes, "Despite having the power to control everything, God voluntarily limits the exercise of that power. . . . Almighty could mean all-determining control or it could mean a power that does not monopolize but delegates power. And, given the reality of evil in the world, God's delegation of power seems completely undeniable." Pinnock, *Most Moved Mover*, 95–96.

15. Ibid., 94–95, emphasis mine.

The power of the triune God is *omnipotent love*. . . . The love of God made known supreme in the cross of Christ has all the power necessary to accomplish the divine purpose of creating and redeeming the world and bringing it to its appointed goal. Because God's omnipotent love is God's own, it does not work by domination or coercion but is sovereign and effective without displacing or bludgeoning God's creatures.[16]

This potency of divine love is very different from the kind of brute power many traditionally associate with omnipotence! As Alister McGrath points out,

In an age which has become increasingly suspicious of the idea of "power," it is perhaps refreshing to be reminded that talk about "God almighty" does not necessarily imply that God is a tyrant, but that God chooses to stand alongside people in their powerlessness.[17]

God's affinity with the powerless is expressed most vividly at the cross, the very antithesis of absolute divine power. It is toward this crucified Trinitarian God that we turn our attention next. As we journey onward into the problem of suffering, the Christian should always have the potent image of the crucifix in his or her mind.

Introducing the Trinity

Tertullian (ca. 160–225) asked the famous question: "What has Athens to do with Jerusalem?" We have already seen features of Greek philosophy embedded within the God of classical theism. The Christian doctrine of the Trinity paints a very different picture, or at least one with a very different emphasis. While the seeds of this doctrine are in the New Testament, it did not become formalized until the church councils in the fourth century when, with much debate, the traditional Nicene Creed was established. This section briefly explores the development of the doctrine of the Trinity, its demise in the Enlightenment, and its resurgence in the last century. Obviously, this is extremely important for a *Christian* understanding of God, God's relationship with creation, and—as we will see later—the problem of suffering.

16. Migliore, *Faith Seeking Understanding*, 86, emphasis mine.
17. McGrath, *Christian Theology*, 212.

Biblical and Historical Considerations

The Hebrew *Shema* affirms the monotheism of Judaism: "Hear, O Israel; The Lord (YHWH) is our God (*Elohim*), the Lord alone (or 'the Lord is one')."[18] In the context of Old Testament times, the *Shema* affirms the worship of YHWH *alone*. The prophets repeatedly called the people to stop worshiping other gods and return to the one true God. As Isaiah states of the Lord: "I am the first and I am the last; besides me there is no god" (Isa 44:6b). The transcendence of the Creator God (YHWH) is evident in the Old Testament, but there are also strong indications of his immanence within creation in the various writers' usage of "spirit," "wisdom," and "word." The spirit of God (literally, "breath" or "wind") is the power by which God animates creation (Gen 2:7) and anoints special people, such as prophets and the coming Messiah.[19] The wisdom of God is more clearly personified in Proverbs 8–9 as "Lady Wisdom," the one who helped YHWH create and structure the world.[20] And the word/voice of God that we hear in Genesis 1 is powerful and effective; such speech-acts reflect that what God says will most definitely come to be.[21]

The New Testament assumes this Old Testament conception of God, but its writers adapt their understanding of God in the light of the Christ-event. Theologians are quick to point out that the (eventual) Trinitarian doctrine does not cancel out Old Testament monotheism, but it does qualify that strict understanding of monotheism significantly.[22] For the Christian,

18. Deut 6:4; Jesus recites the *Shema* in Mark 12:29. There is much revealed in a name: "*Elohim*" is the most common name for God in the Hebrew Scriptures. Its Semitic root "*El*" is in keeping with more general names for God and it can be qualified, such as *El Shaddai* meaning "God Almighty" (Gen 17:1). The personal, covenantal name for God is *Yahweh* (or YHWH, the four consonants or Tetragrammaton, since ancient Hebrew did not possess vowels), and is typically translated as Lord in English Bibles. It was this name for God that was—and is—unspoken by pious Jews. This name was first given to Moses in the burning bush incident (Exod 3:14). There God revealed himself as "I am who I am," or "I will be what I will be," so informing Moses of his faithfulness and presence from generation to generation. See Plantinga et al., *Christian Theology*, 79–80.

19. See also Isa 42:1–3; Ezek 37:1–14.

20. See also Prov 1:20–23; 9:1–6.

21. See also Ps 147:15–20; Isa 55:10–11. It is important to appreciate "the Word *became* flesh" (John 1:14) in this context.

22. Keith Ward states, "The idea of the Trinity does not supersede monotheism; it interprets it, in the light of a specific set of revelatory events and experiences." Ward, "Creation and the Trinity," in Holtzen and Sirvent, *By Faith and Reason*, 99.

there is one, true, Creator God, but this Creator God is the Father, Son, and Holy Spirit together.[23]

The Greek word for "God" is *theos* and it is often associated with God the Father in the New Testament; *kyrios*, the word for "Lord," is often linked with Jesus.[24] The two can be used in close conjunction as, for example, in Philippians 2:9–11:

> Therefore God (*theos*) also highly exalted him [Jesus] and gave him the name that is above every name, so that at the name of Jesus every knee should bend, in heaven and on earth and under the earth, and every tongue should confess that Jesus Christ is Lord (*kyrios*), to the glory of God (*theos*) the Father.

And again in 1 Corinthians 8:4–6:

> We know that . . . "there is no God (*theos*) but one" . . . yet for us there is one God (*theos*), the Father, from whom all things came and for whom we exist; and one Lord (*kyrios*), Jesus Christ, through whom are all things and through whom we exist.

There are clearly echoes of the *Shema* in Paul's Christology.[25] While the close Father-Son connection is mentioned frequently in the New Testament, that same intimacy does not often include the Holy Spirit.[26] Given, however, the earlier Old Testament usage of spirit, word, and wisdom as the means by which a transcendent God relates with the world, it is perhaps not such a huge step in thinking for the New Testament authors to link the

---

23. Plantinga et al., *Christian Theology*, 82. They later make clear that "scholars agree that the Bible does not contain the formal *doctrine* of the Trinity in any explicit fashion. One certainly cannot point to a single biblical text that declares [the Trinity] as clearly as [in] the Athanasian Creed. . . . But the Bible in its unfolding narrative, and therefore progressive revelation, does imply the Trinitarian conception of God, the vectors of which, upon reflection on the Bible as a whole, are systematized by the church's ecumenical confessions." Ibid., 111, their emphasis.

24. *Kyrios* had other *political* connotations in that Caesar claimed the title "Lord." To a first-century Jewish Christian, therefore, "Jesus is Lord" is an affirmation of Jesus being linked to the most personal Old Testament name for God (YHWH) *and* a rejection of their allegiance to the Roman Empire.

25. Sampley, "1 Corinthians," 897–98.

26. In 2 Cor 13:13 and Matt 28:19 the three are mentioned together in the context of the practical life of the church. There is also significant discussion of the Holy Spirit in John 14, a critical passage in developing a theology of the Holy Spirit. For an introduction, see Hauerwas and Willimon, *Holy Spirit*.

person of Jesus the Messiah with God's word and wisdom, and the person of the Holy Spirit with the divine spirit.[27]

By means of an illustrative christological segue, Colossians 1:15–17 eloquently states the following concerning Jesus:

> He is the image of the invisible God, the firstborn of all creation; for in him all things in heaven and on earth were created, things visible and invisible, whether thrones or dominions or rulers or powers—all things have been created through him and for him. He himself is before all things, and in him all things hold together.

The same sentiments are further echoed in Hebrews 1:3:[28]

> He is the reflection of God's glory and the exact imprint of God's very being, and he sustains all things by his powerful word.

A graphic illustration of Christ as "the image (Gk. *icon*) of the invisible God" is the mathematical form of an ellipse. If you place a point source of light at one focus of a closed elliptical mirror, the light rays will all reflect off the curved surface and form an image at the other focus. The optical properties of the ellipse result in a *perfect* image of the source, free from any aberrations. This analogy works extremely well for the Father and Son—but, sadly, omits the Spirit.

The subsequent phrase in Colossians 1:15, "the firstborn of all creation," leads us to the well-known Arian controversy. Arius of Alexandria (ca. 250–336), who emphasized a strict monotheistic understanding of God, held that Christ could not, therefore, share the same divine nature. Instead, Christ was "created by the Father's will for the purpose of mediating between the eternal, immutable, unknowable God and the temporal, suffering, searching world—a metaphysical bridge between God and humanity."[29] Arius, citing Scripture and utilizing logic, argued that Jesus was not coeternal with the Father—"there was when he was not"—and was hence *subordinate* to the Father.[30] This christological controversy was addressed at the first ecumenical Council of Nicaea in 325 CE. It was there

---

27. Plantinga et al., *Christian Theology*, 112–14.

28. See also John 1:1–5.

29. Ibid., 122.

30. Mark Noll points out, "Arius was careful not to say 'there was *a time* when the Son was not,' since Arius conceded that the Son had been begotten before time began." Noll, *Turning Points*, 45, his emphasis. Note: "begotten, not made" makes the rebuttal explicit in the Nicene Creed.

that the bishops declared that Christ the Son was indeed "of the *same* essence/substance" (Gk. *homoousios*) with God the Father.[31] It was, then, the rise of theological disputes that led to the formal doctrine of the Trinity and the consequent rendering of alternative views as inadequate or, pejoratively, as heretical. But this complex matter was hardly settled at Nicaea.[32] This was, in part, because of subtle ambiguities in the meanings of key Greek and Latin words, and their wider connotations. Then, as now, we struggle with the choice of words because of their meaning(s). After all, how can the Divine be expressed in human language that derives all its analogies and metaphors from the physical world?

An earlier related issue was that of modalism. Understandably, the oneness of God was deemed paramount. So how do you then incorporate Christ, the divine Word (John 1:1–3, 14), into a monarchical Godhead? Modalism's response was to deny any real, enduring personal distinction between Father, Son, and Spirit.[33] Instead such differences were merely divine manifestations or behavioral "modes." Consequently God in Godself is genuinely one person, but is merely operating *as* Creator (Father), *as* Redeemer (Son), and *as* Sanctifier (Spirit) *within* cosmic history. This use of language indicates the *unreal* nature of the manifestations. Modalism, then, maintains that the one God is genuinely unknowable because God cannot be communicated apart from this talk of modes.

Tertullian of Carthage (ca. 160–225) countered that opinion: the Father, Son, and Spirit *were* distinct or discrete, yet *not* separate or independent of each other. They had the same *substance* or *essence* (Gk. *ousia*), but three "persons" (Latin *persona*, Gk. *prosopon*). In this context, it is important to know that *persona* literally means a "mask" (or a "face"). Moreover, Roman actors used various masks to enable the audience to identify which character or role they were playing. Alister McGrath comments, "It is quite possible that Tertullian wanted his readers to understand the idea of 'one substance, three persons' to mean that God played three *distinct yet related*

---

31. Greek: *ousios* = substance, essence; alternatively, "of the same substance" or consubstantial (Latin *substantia*).

32. For further details, see Chadwick, *Early Church*, 125–51.

33. Plantinga et al., *Christian Theology*, 119. Alister McGrath points out there are two forms of modalism: *chronological* and *functional*. Chronological modalism has God appearing as Father, Son, or Spirit *sequentially* in history. This view is also referred to as Sabellianism, after Sabellius (early third century). Functional modalism holds that God functions in three different ways at the same moment in time. See McGrath, *Christian Theology*, 244–45.

roles in the great drama of human redemption."[34] Regardless of original connotations associated with the meaning of *persona*, the word "person" creates tensions and confusion for us. We tend to associate the term with "individuality." McGrath clarifies the distinction in this way:

> For early Christian writers, the word "person" is an expression of the individuality of a human being, *as seen in his or her words and actions*. Above all, *there is an emphasis upon the idea of social relationships*. A person is someone who plays a role in social drama, who relates to others. . . . "Individuality" does not imply social relationships, whereas "personality" relates to the part played by an individual in a web of relationships, by which that person is perceived to be distinctive by others.[35]

In light of that, the Trinity—a term invented by Tertullian—is *not* to be imagined as three *individuals*, or tritheism.

Origen (ca. 185–254) developed this "person" idea further and also affirmed that the Son and the Spirit were never at any time nonexistent.[36] This is important as it introduces the notions of what we today term the "economic" and "immanent" Trinity.[37] The former is the God who is known *through* God's acts *in history*—in salvation and in creation, as Tertullian emphasized. The latter is the Trinitarian God *beyond* created space and time, or the Godhead's essential interrelation apart from creation. In this, Origen was truly a pioneer, as he essentially anticipated later Trinitarian orthodoxy developed around the Council of Constantinople (381 CE).

In summary, modalism recognizes the Son's full deity but *subsumes* him into a single monarchical Godhead. In contrast, Arianism recognizes the full personhood of Christ, but *subordinates* him to God the Father, thereby making him distinctly inferior. As mentioned earlier, these nuanced, multifaceted issues were not resolved at Nicaea. The term *homoousios* could be seen as supporting modalism. Many in the East preferred the term *homoiousios*—"of *similar* substance"—to highlight the personal distinctions between the Father and Son, without compromising their

34. McGrath, *Christian Theology*, 240, emphasis mine.

35. Ibid., 200, emphasis mine.

36. Another important Greek word was that of *hypostasis*. Originally it was synonymous with *homoousios* (of the same substance/essence) but came to mean the same as *prosopon* (i.e., a distinct individual existence in the Godhead). Plantinga et al., *Christian Theology*, 121–23.

37. Greek *oikonomia* = economy; it means, in this context, the divine ordering of the affairs of creation and salvation.

deity.[38] But this was also problematic as *homoiousios* would be welcomed by Arians to justify their position, which goes to show how much difference one Greek letter (*i*—iota) can make! In the end, Athanasius (ca. 295–373), along with the influential Cappadocian Fathers (Basil of Caesarea, Gregory of Nyssa, and Gregory of Nazianzus), resolved this critical linguistic and theological matter. They claimed that Arius was interpreting Scripture too selectively and too literally in his proof-texting. Athanasius argued that such verses needed to be seen in the overall theological context of Scripture and not in isolation. Together, they concluded *homoousios*, rightly understood, could be used to reject both modalism and Arianism. These views were eventually formalized in the Nicene-Constantinopolitan Creed at the 381 CE Ecumenical Council.[39] They also (finally!) clarified the status of the Holy Spirit, recognizing his personhood, deity, and coequality, so establishing a truly *Trinitarian* doctrine.

In conclusion, the Eastern Fathers approached the doctrine of the Trinity by first emphasizing the differentiation of the three persons, followed by their unity of divine essence or nature. This view therefore stresses the *relational* character of the Trinity. In contrast, the Western Church, through Augustine and, later, Thomas Aquinas, highlighted the Trinity's unity with the different persons playing a secondary role. This subtle—but not insignificant—distinction had real consequences for the history of the Eastern and Western Churches. The doctrine of the Trinity's resurgence in the West during the last century, together with a reawakening of a theology of the Holy Spirit, is—in no small part—a recognition of the Eastern priorities.

The Social Trinity

St. Augustine (354–430) proposed a number of metaphors to portray the Trinity. One was a love analogy with a Lover, the Beloved, and the bond of love between them—the triplet corresponding to the Father, Son, and Spirit. Not only is there an obvious hierarchy present, but the depersonalized Spirit is hardly a coequal member of the triplet. Richard of St. Victor in Paris (d. 1173), again building on the foundational text "God is Love" (1 John 4:8), proposed another analogy—one that was unusual for the

---

38. Chadwick, *Early Church*, 141–42; Plantinga et al., *Christian Theology*, 122–26.

39. This is commonly called the Nicene Creed in liturgy, but it is more explicit and detailed than the original 325 CE creed.

Western Church. He stressed the logic of love necessitated a *plurality* of divine persons and required at least three equal persons, since he believed that the *shared* love of two for a third was more noble than the love between just two persons. Earlier in the East, John of Damascus (ca. 676–749) introduced an influential new term to describe the Trinity: *perichoresis*. This Greek word means "reciprocal indwelling" or "mutual interpenetration." In other words: a dynamic community, and stresses the unity of the three persons as "beings-in-relationship." As Alister McGrath puts it, "The concept of *perichoresis* allows the individuality of the persons to be maintained, while insisting that each person shares in the life of the other two."[40] Rather than an emphasis on self-sufficiency, there is interdependence within the Trinitarian life. This unique unity of purpose, fellowship, and love within the divine communion counters the criticism of tritheism.

There have been numerous other attempts at metaphors for the Trinity: water (ice, liquid, steam); family (father, mother, child); egg (yoke, white, shell); music (source, score, sound); a three-cord rope or braid, a shamrock, etc. But all are found lacking to one degree of another, as they all tend toward either modalism or tritheism. This is the problem of visualization.[41] The resulting tendency is therefore to either wrap the Trinity in unfathomable mystery, or to simply dismiss it as incoherent. This latter view grew in prominence with the rise of Rationalism during the Enlightenment.

As science gained in stature, God as *Creator* became an impersonal deity—rather than God as *Father*. As we saw earlier with deism, God became—at best—merely the Instigator of the universe and had no further involvement in creation. The doctrine of the Trinity was not only deemed incoherent, but also impractical. Immanuel Kant (1724–1804) said,

> The doctrine of the trinity, taken literally, has *no practical relevance at all*, even if we think we understand it; and it is even more clearly irrelevant if we realize that it transcends all our concepts. Whether we are to worship three or ten persons in the divinity makes no

40. McGrath, *Christian Theology*, 241. Anthony Thiselton also points out, "The Trinity has immediate pastoral relevance because in God the self is *not an isolated self-centered being* but a *self-in-relation to others*." Thiselton, *Systematic Theology*, 36, his emphasis.

41. There is a similar visualization problem in quantum mechanics. If you try to visualize the results of the Schrodinger equation for an atom, you end up with "images" that are inadequate because they are based on analogies from the macroscopic world of classical physics. The language *is* mathematical and in that tongue the quantum description is coherent, elegant, *and* practical. There is, among physicists, a recognition of the futility of trying to visualize such mathematics, while appreciating its beauty and simplicity.

difference . . . this distinction can make no difference in [the student's] conduct.[42]

Thomas Jefferson (1743–1826), Founding Father and third president of the United States, articulated his annoyance on the apparent irrationality of the Trinity in a letter to Timothy Pickering, dated February 27, 1821:

> No one sees with greater pleasure than myself the progress of reason in its advances towards rational Christianity. When we shall have done away the incomprehensible jargon of the Trinitarian arithmetic, that three are one, and one is three; when we shall have knocked down the artificial scaffolding, reared to mask from view the simple structure of Jesus, when, in short, we shall have unlearned everything which has been taught since his day, and got back to the pure and simple doctrines he inculcated, we shall then be truly and worthily his disciples: and my opinion is that if nothing had ever been added to what flowed purely from His lips, the whole world would at this day have been Christian.[43]

Christians today, if we are honest, can appreciate the points raised by both Kant and Jefferson. The Trinity, as Roderick Leupp—borrowing from Winston Churchill—puts it, "is viewed as a riddle wrapped up inside a puzzle and buried in an enigma."[44] Mystery notwithstanding, we need to ask questions, to probe and see if we can thereby gain a better understanding of our faith—including the Trinity. As St. Anselm reminds us, faith by its very nature seeks understanding.

The influential Roman Catholic theologian Karl Rahner (1904–84) was right to lament: "Despite their orthodox confession of the Trinity, Christians are, in their practical life, almost mere 'monotheists.'"[45] The "Father of Modern Theology," Friedrich Schleiermacher (1768–1834), relegated the Trinity to the status of an appendix to theology. Karl Barth (1886–1968), on the other hand, nested the Trinity at the very beginning of his magisterial

42. Kant, *Conflict of the Faculties*, 65–67, his emphasis.

43. Thomas Jefferson to Timothy Pickering. See http://founders.archives.gov/documents/Jefferson/98-01-02-1870.

44. Leupp, *Knowing the Name of God*, 16.

45. Rahner, *Trinity*, 10. He continues, "We must be willing to admit that, should the doctrine of the Trinity have to be dropped as false, the major part of religious literature could well remain virtually unchanged." Ibid., 10–11. I would add that even those who hold a "high" Christology, and so recognize the divinity of Christ, are often *functionally* "binitarians," with the dove of the Spirit having flown away.

Church Dogmatics.[46] For Barth, the Trinity is not a puzzle that is required to be solved, but an explanatory framework which sets theology in its proper perspective, and thus offers solutions to its problems and riddles.[47] And so began a resurgence in Trinitarian scholarship in the twentieth century, one that begins with God's self-revelation.

In 1970 Rahner proposed an axiomatic rule, namely, "The economic Trinity is the immanent Trinity, and vice versa." What this means is that God *revealed* to us in *history* as Father (Creator), Son (Redeemer), and Holy Spirit (Sanctifier)—the economic Trinity—*is* truly who God is apart from creation, in other words God's essential nature—the immanent Trinity.[48] This rule was to counter the tendency of primarily seeing God as One and then tacking on the Trinity afterward, or regarding the Trinity as a manifestation—or the operation—of the One God *within* cosmic history (i.e., modalism), rather than in actuality from all eternity. Instead we start with divine revelation—the biblical witness and our experience of God's "economy" in salvation history—rather than beginning with the "god-of-the-philosophers" or natural theology. Centrally, it is Jesus—God's Word—who reveals to us the nature of God. It is through Jesus the Messiah and the life-giving Spirit that we *know* God. Consequently, it is only from this post-resurrection starting point, in conjunction with further theological reflection, that we are able to formulate the doctrine of the immanent Trinity. Harold Wells summarizes the situation well:

> The theology of the immanent Trinity and the perichoretic relations of the three Persons should not be taken to mean that the mystery of God's triunity is entirely known to us. God as Trinity remains a mystery. . . . When we speak of the Father begetting

46. Plantinga et al., *Christian Theology*, 129; McGrath, *Christian Theology*, 252.

47. Ibid., 253.

48. These three actions are not exclusively differentiated to the three persons. To ensure divine unity the balancing rule is: "All of the acts of the triune God in the world are indivisible." Hence the Father does not act alone in creation, or the Son in the work of redemption, or the Spirit alone in the work of sanctification. See Migliore, *Faith Seeking Understanding*, 71. Furthermore, Keith Ward cautions, "One can insist . . . that the economic Trinity, God known to us historically through Christ and in the power of the Spirit, gives an insight into what God truly is. It is our only access to what has been called the imminent Trinity, the inner Trinitarian being of God, and such access is authentic and reliable. . . . [However,] it is not that there is no more to God than what is revealed to us, nor that we know exactly what God's inner being is like when we speak of the Trinity. It is rather that God essentially is such as to be authentically revealed as a Trinitarian God." Ward, "Creation and the Trinity," in Holtzen and Sirvent, *By Faith and Reason*, 101.

the Son, and of the Spirit proceeding from the Father, and of the three mutually indwelling one another, we speak biblically, or at least in a manner congruent with the Bible—but we do not know exactly what we say! . . . We may ask, then, whether it is important to speak of the mystery of the immanent Trinity at all. Have we moved beyond our ability to know? . . . Though aware of the limitations of our knowledge, we are not agnostics about God. We believe we really do know God, not because we are naturally capable of it but because God has gifted us with a share of God's own self-knowledge. This knowledge is basic to confident faith and hope, essential to confident preaching, to heartfelt worship, and to committed following.[49]

The contemporary renaissance in Western Trinitarian thought has resulted in a more personal, dynamic, and relational tone—affirming traditional insights from the Eastern Church. Jürgen Moltmann introduced the influential view of the "social Trinity" where God is like a family; a loving community with differentiated persons. Understandably, this view is subject to the criticism of tritheism due to the relative independence of the persons within the social Trinity. Just as in the fourth century, the debates are not only theological and philosophical, but on the meaning and connotations of words. Harold Wells astutely points out that our assumed Western notion of personhood is also part of the problem:

> It is not that we need a less relational view of the triune God as an eternal communion of love; rather, we need a less individualistic and more relational view of human personhood as intimate interdependence and mutuality. This is more a life-giving and liberating doctrine of God . . . and, I suggest, closer to the biblical witness to Jesus, one with his *Abba* and the Spirit.[50]

The *perichoretic* unity, mentioned earlier, is therefore paramount in the social Trinity. This resonates with Christ's High Priestly Prayer in John 17:20–23 (emphasis added):

> I ask not only on behalf of these [disciples], but also on behalf of those who will believe in me through their word, that they may all be one. *As you, Father, are in me and I am in you*, may they also be in us, so that the world may believe that you have sent me. The glory that you have given me I have given them, so that they may be one, *as we are one*, I in them and you in me, that they may

49. Wells, *Christic Center*, 176–77.

50. Ibid., 179.

become completely one, so that the world may know that you have
sent me and have loved them even as you have loved me.

In conclusion, the Orthodox view is that the Son is eternally being
generated (or "begotten") and the Spirit is eternally "breathed out" (*spirate*)
or being sent ("proceeding") from the Father, the fount of divinity. There is,
then, forever a "package deal" in the divine dance: Father, Son, and Spirit,
united in purpose, fellowship, and love. Like Moltmann, the Greek Orthodox theologian John Zizioulas also emphasizes the reality of this social
communion. If the Trinity is fundamentally a *communion*, a shared life of
beings-in-relationship, then we too need to be in healthy relationships with
God, each other, and creation. Communion, therefore, is what *being*—life
itself—is all about. In light of this, we have to reexamine *all* our theologies,
such as our views on atonement, the church, mission, and worship.[51]

This chapter has briefly explored the topic of the Trinity and has emphasized mutual relationship, rather than divine power, and has endeavored
to balance cohesion with differentiation. For some, this matter will still be
very confusing despite my best efforts! Recall, then, that for Karl Barth,
"the Trinity was not a puzzle that requires to be solved, but an explanatory framework which sets theology in its proper perspective."[52] Reconsider
too the eloquent words of Richard Rohr at the beginning of this chapter.[53]
Nevertheless, I appreciate that some may ask: "How do I progress forward
from here?" Speaking pragmatically, then, I recommend erring on the side
of a *relational* Trinity with distinctive persons, rather than on the side of
an imperial Divine. Our Western history has, for many centuries, been too
closely associated with the latter, resulting in a God who is perceived to be
silent and distant by many. Both our cultural and Christian heritages are
still heavily influenced by this negative legacy of deism, as we will see in
coming chapters. In countering *that* view of God, whose roots lay in classical theism, a nuanced Trinitarian community is a much healthier option
for the church and the world in the twenty-first century.

What God wants?

---

51. See McGrath, *Christian Theology*, 261–64.

52. Ibid., 253.

53. See also Rohr, *Divine Dance*, and Hauerwas and Willimon, *Holy Spirit*, 1–31.

3

The Crucified God

When the crucified Jesus is called "the image of the invisible God," the meaning
is that *this* is God, and God is like *this*.

—Jürgen Moltmann

Meanings of the Cross

The child's innocent question, "Why did Jesus *have to* die?" is one
that sends a shudder of fear to any parent, grandparent, or Sunday
school teacher! In considering an age-appropriate response, what
should we tell the inquisitive child? Regardless of *what* we say, our reply
will reveal something about how *we* view the character of God in the face
of human suffering. There are many different responses to this question
and, as we will see, each of them is culturally located. Our understanding
of the person and work of Jesus is made evident in the way we think about
his death. The New Testament writers were also trying to answer the same
question to first-century Jews and non-Jews using language and images that
were culturally familiar. They all knew, of course, that ultimately it was the
Romans who crucified Jesus.[1] His radical teachings were perceived to be a

---

1. Indeed, it was the Jewish and Greco-Roman perceptions of death by crucifixion—
namely, it was scandalous—that created a credibility problem for Paul's mission: "We

threat to the religious and political stability of the region. But the bodily resurrection of Jesus witnessed by his followers demanded an explanation as to the added significance of his death.

Some New Testament writers portray Jesus as paying the ransom price to liberate—or *redeem*—a slave in the secular marketplace (Mark 10:45; 1 Cor 6:20; 1 Tim 2:5–6). This is also mirrored in the exodus: deliverance *from* bondage and slavery in Egypt *by* the blood of the Passover lamb *into* the promised land (albeit via the wilderness). It is no surprise, then, that the author of Hebrews gave his explanation using the Jewish religious symbolism of sacrifice (Heb 9:26; 10:10, 12; see also 1 Cor 5:7). The same author also speaks of Christ as the "mediator of a new covenant" (Heb 8:6; 9:15; 12:24), not only paralleling Moses, but in the priestly role of intermediary between God and his people (Heb 4:14–16; 8:1). Other writers place Jesus' death in the context of a cosmic conflict between good and evil, between God and the "principalities and powers" (Col 2:15; Eph 6:12; Heb 2:14–15; 1 John 3:8). We will explore some of these metaphors briefly in a moment. Evidently, Scripture does not present a unique, timeless, or universal "answer" to the child's probing question; the appeal of each response is determined by the context of the audience (e.g., Jew, non-Jew, slave, and free person).

It seems to have escaped many Western Christians' attention that we do not live in first-century Palestine—at least that is the impression I get from listening to sermons and participating in Bible studies! We, today, do not think in terms of routinely offering ritual sacrifice or of purchasing slaves in a marketplace. Moreover, our culture does not think in dualistic terms of Satan and his demons in a continuing cosmic duel with God. Thinking in such terms was appropriate when such social practices and overarching worldviews were culturally helpful analogies. Since they are not featured in modern worldviews, those metaphors have lost their explanatory power in helping us understand the significance of Jesus' death. They have some benefit, of course, if we try to think in first-century terms, but that can ever only be partial and unsatisfying for *today's* Christian. The significance of the cross needs to be seen afresh in every time and culture. This is nothing new, and church history is littered with examples of new ways to interpret the cross and make it socially relevant—a process that continues today. I will briefly consider three traditional responses to the

---

proclaim Christ crucified, a stumbling block to Jews and foolishness to Gentiles" (1 Cor 1:23).

"Why did Jesus have to die?" question. In so doing, be alert as to what these viewpoints tell us about God's character and actions. This is foundational for our understanding of God and suffering.

We will start with the so-called *Christus Victor* ("Christ the Victor") model, in which the basic premise is that the universe is a battleground between good and evil.[2] We live within a cosmic war zone with God and his angels fighting against Satan and his demons, who are holding humanity and the natural order in captivity. Jesus gets caught up in this epic war and is killed; God is thereby defeated and Satan (seemingly) gets the victory. Christ's resurrection overturns Satan's short-lived success, giving God control of the universe and liberating everything that was under Satan's power. How precisely the death and resurrection of Jesus results in humanity's salvation is not clear.[3] But the outcome is: the devil and his cohorts are defeated, death's power is overturned, and Christ is the victor.

Closely allied with *Christus Victor* is the "ransom model." The patristic fathers, Irenaeus, Tertullian, Origen, and—most notably—Gregory of Nyssa (ca. 335–95), developed this image. Since the Fall, Satan has held humankind in captivity. Gregory's high regard for divine justice meant that God was required to acknowledge Satan's rights over sinful humanity as being legitimate. Nevertheless, God devised a redemptive plan analogous to a financial transaction in a slave market. The *perfect human* Jesus was an appealing ransom to the devil in exchange for sinful humanity. Gregory of Nyssa portrays Christ as God's bait dangling on a fish hook that the devil—the ravenous sea monster—swallows.[4] Satan was both fooled and caught; Satan did not recognize the deity (the hook) hidden under the guise of human nature. Divine life and light entered into the domain of death and darkness, and overcame it—for Satan cannot enslave the divine Son of God. That Satan had unwittingly overreached his powers became apparent when Christ's divinity was revealed in the resurrection and Satan lost his grasp on captive humanity. While the sensibility of divine justice may have

2. See Aulén, *Christus Victor*.

3. Alister McGrath comments, "Aulén's [*Christus Victor*] approach . . . offered no rational justification for the manner in which the forces of evil are defeated through the cross of Christ. Why the cross? Why not through some other manner?" McGrath, *Christian Theology*, 325–26. He also observes, "In one sense, [*Christus Victor*] is not a 'theory of atonement.' It is much more an expression of confidence in the difference that Christ's death and resurrection have made." Ibid., 322–23.

4. Sea monsters represent the forces of chaos in Old Testament times; this can be linked to Satan in New Testament times.

been preserved in this speculative model, nevertheless God is evidently a trickster who is prepared to use his Son to lure Satan![5]

Satan is prominent in both the ransom and cosmic warfare models, and in both Christ is victorious. For this reason, I merge these two metaphors here, even though their ways of dealing with Satan are different. *Christus Victor's* dualistic rhetoric is in keeping with the apocalyptic thinking of the time. Moreover, until Emperor Constantine, the church was in territories under Roman occupation and, from time-to-time, experienced persecution. Consequently, this popular notion of a triumphant Christ would resonate within such a society and give hope for oppressed communities that needed liberation—the same is true today. But if you think about this picture for a moment, it is clear we have little or no role to play. In this cosmic conflict, humans are essentially spectators; we are victims, or hostages, who need liberating. It is the powers (e.g., fear, death, devil, etc.) that hold the cosmos in bondage. In the final victory God rescues the world from its captivity and restores it. Or, in the words of Paul: "In Christ God was reconciling the world (Gk. *cosmos*) to himself" (2 Cor 5:19).

This model, at least in this classic form, has faded away from our consciousness for a variety of reasons. (a) In the case of ransom, we understandably have an aversion to the idea that God is prepared to resort to deception *and* to use the Son as bait! (b) Many question whether, in fact, the devil had rights of ownership over humanity—does this not undermine divine sovereignty? And does God *negotiate* with the devil? (c) Given the continuing presence of suffering, there is a lack of evidence for this cosmic victory and the resulting reign of God in our world. Putting it another way, does this model lead to the denial of the continuing power of sin and evil in our lives and in history?[6] (d) Modern worldviews, informed in part by science, have no place for a dualistic picture of a cosmic battle between God and Satan. (e) Finally, what happened to human responsibility for the injustice, violence, and evil in the world?

Nevertheless, this model has some merits. It stresses the reality of evil[7] and its power to hold humankind in bondage; we can be addicted to many

---

5. Anthony Thiselton points out the irony of this grotesque image: "The devil had deceived humankind [in the garden of Eden]; so God deceived the devil." He then adds, "But Scripture does not imply that the 'ransom' is 'paid' to anyone: costliness is part of the metaphor, but '*payment to*' is *not*. The ransom is *from* bondage *by* the blood of Christ *to* new creation and life in Christ." Thiselton, *Systematic Theology*, 212, his emphasis.

6. Migliore, *Faith Seeking Understanding*, 183.

7. Note too that Aulén was writing after the horrors of World War I, where humanity's

things in our contemporary culture. The model also correlates with Jesus being the Savior of the World, *whether or not* we accept or respond to that "good news." Moreover, and speaking more broadly, Christ's victory in the resurrection saves the entire cosmos, affirming the essential goodness of creation that God thinks is worth redeeming.[8] For these—and other—reasons, it is no surprise that we have seen a revival of this idea within modern adaptations of the *Christus Victor* model.[9]

St. Anselm (1033–1109) rejected the devil's ownership of humanity and introduced the influential "satisfaction model." This model arose in perilous and uncertain feudal times. He therefore viewed the relationship between God and humankind like that between a medieval lord and his serfs. Since disobedience dishonors the lord, either satisfaction must be given or punishment (ultimately death) must follow. Anselm's satisfaction theory therefore correlates well with the medieval shame and honor system and its sense of duty and indebtedness. For Anselm, to sin is nothing else than to not render God his due, namely perfect loyalty and obedience. Sin is therefore a debt of honor to be repaid (restoration) thereby *satisfying* God's honor.[10] The irony is evident: given the offensive nature of sin, while humanity *must* give this satisfaction, only God *can* provide it.[11] After all, such recompense can only be made by one of equal status. In steps Jesus Christ, the perfect God-man who lives a life of faultless loyalty and obedience. In addition, he *willingly* gives something more; the sinless Christ gives up his own life. Jesus, then, is like a heroic, honorable knight who is killed. In Christ's death, God is obligated to reward Christ, who does not need it since he is perfect. So Jesus passes that gift on to his brothers and sisters (humankind). The final outcome is that God's honor is restored and all humanity is forgiven—but creation's restoration is not mentioned in this saga. This, then, is Anselm's logical explanation as to why it was *necessary* for God to become human.

Cultural distance from feudal society means that we may find this model quaint or bizarre—even irrelevant. Anselm should not be criticized

---

"evil" was self-evident, thereby countering the optimism of the Enlightenment.

8. This being the case, it is clearly inconsistent to promote *Christus Victor* along with an escapist eschatology in which heaven is a place of disembodied spirits!

9. For example, see Weaver, *Nonviolent Atonement*.

10. This begs the question: If God is impassible, how can God *suffer* the dishonor of humanity's sin?

11. Migliore, *Faith Seeking Understanding*, 184.

for that, though, as all models are culturally contextualized. But we can ask: "Is God's behavior *really* analogous to that of a medieval lord?" Does his honor really need satisfying? By *us*? If a debt is owed to God, why can't God simply forgive it? After all, that is—so the gospel writers tell us—precisely what Jesus counsels *us* to do?[12] All this paints God as one who is easily slighted for things fallible humans cannot help but do. It also seems unsatisfactory that the cultural shame and honor system dictates how God must act! Moreover, is God not a God of *grace* and *mercy*? As Daniel Migliore points out,

> Grace is made conditional on satisfaction. But is conditional grace still grace? According to the New Testament, it is not God but humanity who needs to be reconciled. In the New Testament God is not so much the object as the subject of reconciliation in Christ.[13]

Furthermore, while Anselm locates the problem as one between God and humanity (not Satan), what is *our* role in the satisfaction model? Nothing. Ultimately this is an arrangement between God and Jesus, the incarnate Son, who alone can save us.[14] Finally, does this emphasis on honor imply that the powers that hold people in bondage (all too self-evident in medieval times) are therefore unreal? Despite such criticisms, Anselm's satisfaction model was a remarkable and influential achievement in both Protestant and Roman Catholic theology.

John Calvin describes a variety of redemption metaphors in his *Institutes* within the context of Christ as prophet, priest (or mediator), and king.[15] One key perspective is that of Christ being a willing sacrifice to "appease the wrath of God." According to God's own law, our sin (anything less than perfection) demands *punishment*—death. God nevertheless still loves the world and, according to Calvin, graciously initiates a way to rescue sinful humankind while ensuring that the legal penalty for disobedience is still satisfied. Building on the Hebrew image of sacrifice, the sinless Messiah carries on himself (analogous to a scapegoat) the sin, guilt, and shame of the whole world. The manner of Christ's brutal death as a condemned (cursed) *criminal*, though he is in fact innocent, makes redemption a *penal*

---

12. Heim, *Saved from Sacrifice*, 25.

13. Migliore, *Faith Seeking Understanding*, 184.

14. A positive feature is that Anselm links the atoning *work* of Christ to Christology, the *person* of Christ.

15. Calvin's *Institutes* represents the foundation of Reformation systematic theology; see bk. 2, chs. 15 and 16.

substitutionary act. The death of Jesus for Calvin is, then, not to be understood in terms of satisfying God's honor, but God's justice. The sinless Christ is a *substitute for our punishment*. We, deserving of God's wrath and death, are acquitted by the perfectly obedient Christ dying in our place.[16] Denny Weaver concludes: "The death of Jesus involved a divinely orchestrated plan through which Jesus' death could satisfy divine justice or divine law in order to save sinful humankind."[17] Mark Heim says the same thing, but more bluntly: "Christ is sent to die so that a merciful God can fulfill the demands of a just God's law."[18]

Since Calvin was first trained as a lawyer, it is perhaps no surprise that his adaption of Anselm's satisfaction model is strongly focused around a legal metaphor and divine justice. Penal substitution emphasizes the rule of law and God as the trial judge. God ensures that the demands of *his own* laws are satisfied. The added irony is this: if you believe—as Calvin did—that God is actively controlling all events in this world, then it follows that God is orchestrating all the evil and then punishes Jesus for it! Even if you don't believe in predestination, this view still promotes a God of violence, since God *requires* punishment and death to affect salvation. Some critics regard penal substitution as divine child abuse. Even if you find that view a harsh caricature, it is still fair to ask: is it *just* to punish the innocent for the sins of others?

Without any solid evidence to support this, I suggest that if you view God as a disciplinarian—as one who tests us, and perhaps even punishes us—then you are likely to believe in penal substitutionary atonement. After all, such a God told Abraham to sacrifice his son Isaac apparently as a test (Gen 22:1–19). This story is one of a number of troubling incidents in the Old Testament, especially if we consider *not* what it says about Abraham and Isaac, but about God himself.[19] If one believes that God was desirous to

16. Note: only the *elect* are redeemed in Calvin's thinking, i.e., those predestined to life with God.

17. Weaver, *Nonviolent Atonement*, 18.

18. Heim, *Saved from Sacrifice*, 25. He adds, "If this is God's wise and compassionate plan for salvation, why does it require such violence? The idea that God sent his Son to be sacrificed for us is indicted here for impugning the moral character of God. We can hardly imagine God demanding the suffering and death of one innocent as the condition of mercy toward guilty others. This tension between wrath and mercy can twist God into a cipher, a dualistic deity who understandably evokes ambiguous responses of both gratitude and fear."

19. This is particularly true when, later in Scripture, we are told that God abhors child sacrifice—see Lev 18:21; 20:1–5; Deut 12:31; 18:10; Jer 7:30–34. Consider also the

test Abraham's faith in this way, it follows quite easily that God would also be prepared to sacrifice his own Son—and even *sent* him to die. A moment of reflection should, I hope, cause us to reject this notion of divine abuse and force us to rethink the meaning of the cross.

Not surprisingly, this sample of traditional atonement metaphors portrays God as an all-powerful ruler, in keeping with the political systems of that day. If such a God is also impassive, as traditionally maintained, then it is hard to see how Jesus and God can be genuinely working together in *unity*. It could be construed as God making kingly demands that a subservient Jesus meekly obeys. These metaphors tend to place God and Jesus on opposite sides, and make God directly *responsible* for Jesus' death. If this is our image of God, then it is no surprise we struggle with such a deity in the face of suffering.

Nowhere in these responses is there a clear affirmation of the Trinity! This traditional doctrine needs to be *explicitly* incorporated into our view of atonement. If not a monarchical God, what undergirds those metaphors is, at best, a totally fragmented Trinity (i.e., tritheism), rather than beings-in-relationship united in purpose and love. A genuinely Trinitarian response to the child's question would not only transform our understanding of the life, death, and resurrection of Jesus, but affirm God's good character. This, I maintain, is the crucial foundation stone from which to build an understanding of God's relationship with a suffering world.

The Crucified God

One Trinitarian atonement metaphor is a modern adaptation of Luther's "Theology of the Cross."[20] According to Douglas John Hall,

> *A Theology of the Cross . . . [is] a statement about God, and what it says about God is* not *that God thinks humankind so wretched that*

troubling notion of God "hardening Pharaoh's heart" (Exod 9:12; 10:1, 20, 27; 11:10) in Pharaoh's contest with Moses, just prior to the exodus. If this truly was the case, which I seriously doubt, Pharaoh's free will was overridden and God was *directly* responsible for the slaughter of all the Egyptian firstborn during the Passover. Put another way: in such circumstances, would it be the act of a just God to hold Pharaoh accountable at the last judgment?

20. Douglas John Hall, leaning on the views of Luther, Kierkegaard, Bonhoeffer (and others), is critical of the sense of triumphalism of Christendom's *theologia gloriae*. In contrast, a "Theology of the Cross" (*theologia crucis*) builds on Christ's death as the prime example of experiential suffering.

it deserves death and hell, but that God thinks humankind and the whole creation so good, so beautiful, so precious in its intention and its potentiality, that its actualization, its fulfillment, its redemption is worth dying for.[21]

Hall's tone is clearly very different from the previous doctrines of reconciliation. God the Father is *not* vindictive; Christ's death is *not* God's plan or God's manipulation of events. Rather, the death of Jesus is a direct consequence of human hate.[22] Mark Heim is equally emphatic: "The elements of violence and punishment [in the crucifixion] are not prescribed and initiated by God."[23] The crucifixion of Jesus can, without doubt, be explored and appreciated on a multitude of levels.[24] But at the most basic level, the death of Jesus was a political act whereby a would-be Messiah was publicly executed, as a deterrent, by the Roman authorities. Crucifixion was a rebellious slave's death; abject humiliation preceded by scourging with whips for a person who had no rights. How one interprets that human tragedy in the light of the resurrection is another matter entirely, as the various New Testament writers elucidate. For example, John's gospel begins with succinct eloquence: "The light shines in the darkness, and the darkness did not overcome it" (John 1:5). Given the type of death, however, the *political* interpretation of the resurrection is that "Jesus is Lord, Caesar is not!"[25] As we know all too well, humankind has a capability for great evil, but God's capability for us is that great good may even come out of our evil intentions and acts.[26] The resurrection of Jesus is the Father and the Spirit's emphatic *NO* to evil having the last word! We will return to this very important aspect in chapter 6.

This allows us to view the cross in a way that removes any tension between Jesus and God the Father. Indeed, if we read the baptism accounts of Jesus in the Synoptic Gospels through a Trinitarian lens, we can recognize the divine unity at the outset of Jesus' ministry—and there is no theological

---

21. Hall, *Cross in Our Context*, 24, his emphasis.

22. Ibid., 103.

23. Heim, *Saved from Sacrifice*, 10.

24. For example, see Rutledge, *Crucifixion*, and Wright, *Jesus and the Victory of God*, 540–611; Wright's arguments are reiterated in *Challenge of Jesus*, 74–95, and—more recently—in *Revolution*.

25. Wright, *Surprised by Hope*, 50.

26. Hall, *Cross in Our Context*, 99.

reason to see that harmony changing.[27] Consequently, Christ's suffering on the cross is also experienced by the Father and the Spirit, but in different ways. If Christ willingly gave himself up to the authorities, then the Father also surrenders himself to the outcome. Jürgen Moltmann writes,

> The Son suffers dying, the Father suffers the death of the Son. The grief of the Father here is just as important as the death of the Son. The Fatherlessness of the Son is matched by the Sonlessness of the Father. . . . The Son suffers in his love being forsaken by the Father as he dies. The Father suffers in his love the grief of the death of the Son. . . . What proceeds from this event between Father and Son is the Spirit which justifies the godless, fills the forsaken with love, and even brings the dead alive.[28]

Trinitarian unity is evident in the Father and Son's submission and mutual separation. Their surrender is not just to the God-given free will of humanity, but to their mission—to do *all* that it takes to save the world. In the process the whole Godhead suffers to bring *shalom* to the all of creation. This shocking, uniquely Christian, claim is—in my view—an underemphasized part of the gospel message.

Insisting on a Trinitarian perspective regardless of the consequences, forces us to reject the traditional doctrines of divine immutability and impassibility. And once we start pulling on the weave of those divine attributes, the absoluteness of the other attributes is also called into question. It is for this reason that some Christians object to a "suffering God," or even—following Luther—to speak more boldly and mystically of a "crucified God." But, as Bonhoeffer puts it, "Only a suffering God can help."[29]

Nicholas Wolterstorff had been convinced for a long time that God was not the impassive, unresponsive, unchanging deity portrayed by classical theologians. But it was in his own experience of profound grief over the death of his twenty-five-year-old son in a mountaineering accident that, through the "prism of tears," he recognized the *suffering* of God. Great grief first requires great love, for grief is suffering the loss of the beloved. In the

---

27. See Matt 3:13–17; Mark 1:9–11; Luke 3:21–22 (and John 1:29–34).

28. Moltmann, *Collected Readings*, 48–49.

29. Cited in Hall, *Cross in Our Context*, 84. Hall adds, "If the crucified one is truly representative of the God by whom faith believes him to have been sent, then, however ponderous the transcendent power that reason and religion have attributed to deity, the Christian God must be seen as the suffering God." Ibid., 85.

intensity of Wolterstorff's personal suffering, that of a father burying his son, he saw the "God of sorrows":

> God is not only the God of the sufferers but the God who suffers. The pain and fallenness of humanity have entered into his heart.... Instead of explaining our suffering God shares it.... God is love. That is why he suffers. To love our suffering sinful world is to suffer.... The one who does not see God's suffering does not see his love. God is suffering love.... The tears of God are the meaning of history.[30]

These deeply moving words from this Yale philosopher-theologian force us to pause and think, particularly for those who have never regarded God the Father—or the Creator God—in such a way.

It follows from theology's emphasis on the mutually indwelling Trinity that at the heart of sin is broken relationship, alienation, and estrangement.[31] This is the essence of the Genesis 3 story and this theme continues throughout the Old Testament to the Babylonian exile. Modernism's myth of progress has underestimated the problem of evil. There is more to evil than meets the eye.[32] For N. T. Wright, evil is the "rebellious idolatry by which humans worship and honor elements of the natural world rather than the God who made them."[33] We are all guilty of that impertinent attitude toward our Creator, beginning with thinking of ourselves as *above* creation. This defiant act puts the *whole* creation "out of joint" in Hebrew thinking, enslaving it and ourselves, leading to death/exile. Evil, then, is that which distorts and defaces creation from what it was meant to be.[34] Hall articulates a similar sentiment and brings in both vertical and horizontal dimensions. Sin "is an *active* nonbeing, a refusal, a rejection, a no to the other: the other who is God, the author of life; the other who is the neighbor, the partner of life; the other that is creation itself, the context of life."[35] In contrast, "the crucified Christ represents the ultimate yes of God

---

30. Wolterstorff, *Lament for a Son*, 81, 90. He adds, "It is said of God that no one can behold his face and live. I always thought this meant that no one could see his splendor and live. A friend said perhaps it meant no one could see his sorrow and live." Ibid., 81.

31. Hall, *Cross in Our Context*, 104.

32. The strength of *Christus Victor*, and its modern variants, is that it takes the scope and power of evil very seriously. See also Wink, *Powers That Be*.

33. Wright, *Surprised by Hope*, 95.

34. Ibid., 95–97.

35. Hall, *Cross in Our Context*, 105, emphasis mine. Hall contrasts "*active* nonbeing" with *passive* nonbeing, which is simply the absence of the good. See also the appendix.

to the human creature, and therefore to creation as a whole."[36] Jesus the Messiah, empowered by the Spirit and affirmed by the Father, comes as the reconciler—the inaugurator of *shalom*, or the rule of God. As a consequence, this life becomes purposeful and authentic as we align our heart, mind, and strength with that of our Creator, Reconciler, and Sanctifier (Deut 6:5; Mark 12:30–31). Moreover, not only is life itself purposed, but so is the cosmos; the goodness of creation is affirmed. Hall states, "The cross of Jesus Christ represents the absolute claim upon the world of the God who created and sustains it, . . . this world is the beloved of God and must not be abandoned."[37] The great Christian hope is ultimately of a redeemed earth; a new creation metaphorically birthed from the old one.[38] The cosmos is made complete and God will live among us (Rev 21:3).

That the triune God thought the whole creation worth dying for is a profound—yet enigmatic—truth. It clearly demonstrates that God is not impassive or immutable, but is willing to take risks—even to suffer a slow, tortuous crucifixion—for the sake of love. Recognizing *God as one who suffers for us, and with us*, allows us to *engage* life, rather than trying to conquer life or control it—as so often has been the goal in the past. We are ever mindful that complete *shalom* is yet to be; God's kingdom is both "now and not yet." Consequently, there is a pervasive eschatological dimension to this theology. Rather than a *fait accompli*, it emphasizes promise, hope, and becoming.[39] But what the resurrection does demonstrate is that the life-giving Spirit wills to give life again. After all, death can only be negated by God (Rom 4:17). Consequently, a theology of the cross—based on faith (not sight), hope (not finality), and love (not power)—sets us free from the anxiety ("sting," 1 Cor 15:54–57) of death itself.[40] All this is "good news" for postmodernity!

In summary, the cross must be placed within the whole historical context of the Christ-event. The Trinitarian mission provides the means for freedom and healing from guilt, shame, and bondage—as well as restored relationships with God, each other, and the physical world around

---

36. Ibid., 99. Wright expresses the same sentiment: The cross is "God's *no* to evil, which then opens the door to *yes* to creation." Wright, *Surprised by Hope*, 87, his emphasis.

37. Hall, *Cross in Our Context*, 220. He adds, "God is committed to [the world] in long-suffering love" (ibid., 224).

38. Wright, *Surprised by Hope*, 103.

39. Hall, *Cross in Our Context*, 30–31.

40. Ibid., 214.

us. Moreover, the Spirit is gradually liberating and transforming those "in Christ" into his nonviolent likeness. It is only in the Christ-event that we can truly understand the meaning of "God is love" (1 John 4:8), for it reveals the heart of the Trinity. God is indeed good. In the Christ-event, something *has* happened, something *is now* happening, and something further *will* happen at Christ's coming (Gk. *parousia*).

We will return to this broad theological theme in chapter 6. The emphasis of these last two chapters has been to stress the importance of a *Trinitarian* worldview. Thinking of the cross from this perspective *unites* the Trinity in suffering, rather than creating an experiential gulf between God the Father and Jesus, which is a tendency of traditional atonement metaphors. Too often Christians feel that *Jesus* can identify with their experience of suffering, but *not* God. This shows the subtle, lingering influence of the traditional doctrine of impassivity and creates a sense of distance between us and God. This distorts, even hinders, our relationship with God—which we depend upon in times of suffering—and is obviously contrary to the ongoing work of the Spirit.

In the next chapter we shift gears completely and consider the presence of suffering in the world that God has made.

•

4

God's Good, Untamed Creation

What a book a devil's chaplain might write on the clumsy, wasteful, blundering, low, and horribly cruel works of nature!

—CHARLES DARWIN

Introduction

Tragically, December 26, 2004, Boxing Day, was a momentous day as it was then that a massive tsunami hit the shores of Indonesia, Sri Lanka, India, and Thailand. Waves up to thirty meters (100 ft.) high hit coastal communities killing a quarter of a million people in more than ten countries. The earthquake that caused this devastation was the third largest ever recorded on a seismograph.[1] While such major catastrophes are relatively rare—not that there is any comfort in that—we were nevertheless reminded once again that we live on a geologically active planet giving rise to volcanoes, earthquakes, and tsunamis. As on January 12, 2010, when an earthquake devastated Haiti, there was an added sense of "unfairness" because the destruction affected some of the poorest regions of the world.

---

1. The fourth-largest occurred on March 11, 2011, just off the coast of northeastern Japan, resulting in a major nuclear incident.

Understandably, these natural disasters make us ask questions about God's sovereignty.

Another turning point in history occurred on All Saints' Day, November 1, 1755, in the city of Lisbon, Portugal. At about 9:30 a.m., a huge earthquake shook the ocean floor, some one hundred miles offshore. When the earthquake occurred, many people were in church celebrating Mass on this important liturgical feast day. Buildings trembled violently; people ran out into the streets praying for mercy as churches, civic buildings, and homes collapsed around them killing thousands. Fires then broke out that were fanned by ferocious winds. Aftershocks reduced to rubble what buildings were left standing. Thousands of survivors made their way to the harbor to seek refuge onboard sailing ships trying to flee the burning city. But then they witnessed the water being mysteriously sucked out of the harbor, revealing old shipwrecks on the seabed, only to watch in shocked disbelief as a wall of water from a tsunami then crashed over them. Many tens of thousands died on that apocalyptic day, which remains the worst single natural disaster in Europe. Where was God when people died on their knees praying to him?[2]

The shock waves continued to affect the cultural, intellectual, and Christian life of Europe long after Lisbon had been destroyed. Despite earlier calamities,[3] this was significantly different; it rocked Christendom. Thomas Long describes the importance:

> Prior to the Enlightenment, natural disasters such as earthquakes, famines, floods, and epidemics were viewed as coming directly from the hand of God. . . . Symbolically, the Lisbon earthquake would be the first disaster of worldwide proportion that could not neatly fit into the accepted idea of divine causality.[4]

The destruction of Lisbon was a major challenge to theology and philosophy at a pivotal historical junction between the old worldview of traditional Christianity, whether Protestant or Roman Catholic, and that of an emerging secular, scientific age. This post–Isaac Newton era was enamored by

---

2. Long, *What Shall We Say?*, 2–18. On Tuesday, September 19, 2017, a powerful (7.1) earthquake caused the roof to collapse during a baptismal service in Santiago the Apostle Catholic Church, Atzala, Mexico. Eleven members of the same family were killed, including two-month-old Elideth Torres de Leon, who was being baptized.

3. The Black Death in the mid-1300s is estimated to have killed up to half of Europe's population.

4. Long, *What Shall We Say?*, 6–7.

science with its clockwork view of the cosmos. Even if faith in a personal deity was not in vogue with the European intelligentsia, many still believed that an omnipotent Creator God kept the world in order. Forty-five years earlier, Leibniz claimed that this particular world was "the best of all possible worlds" that God could have made. In light of Lisbon, Voltaire (in *Candide*) mused, "If this is the best of all possible worlds, what are the others?" In other words, it was no longer easy for reasonable and thoughtful people to see the horrors of Lisbon as the gift of God's "fatherly hand."[5] In Long's view we are all "children of Lisbon," such is the influence of this event. This tragedy changed society because believing in an all-powerful God was deeply challenged by the irrationality and inexplicability of innocent suffering.[6]

Given that Christians proclaim the doctrine of God's *good* creation, how are we to understand the "evils" that arise as a result of natural processes? We will address the complex issue of human free will in the next chapter; just the very mention of the word *Auschwitz* leaves us too stunned and ashamed for words as to the enormity of "moral evil" perpetrated by humankind. We will wrestle first with "natural evil," which seems to create—in many people's minds—a greater problem for belief in God, since it cannot be ascribed to human agency. As we will discover, there is an inevitable overlap between these two chapters because evil is not always so neatly characterized as either natural or moral.[7]

5. Ibid., 16. The reference to God's "fatherly hand" comes from the Heidelberg Confession (1563): "*Question 27:* What do you understand by the providence of God? *Answer:* The almighty and ever-present power of God by which God upholds, as with his hand, heaven and earth and all creatures, and so rules them that leaf and blade, rain and drought, fruitful and lean years, food and drink, health and sickness, prosperity and poverty—*all things, in fact, come to us not by chance but by his fatherly hand*" (emphasis mine). See https://www.crcna.org/welcome/beliefs/confessions/heidelberg-catechism.

6. Long, *What Shall We Say?*, 17. William Hasker adds, "It seems to many of us simply incredible that this world, . . . with all the sordid details of its history, is the best that any world could possibly be." Hasker, *Triumph of God over Evil*, 77. He discusses Leibniz's theodicy at length (see 74–100).

7. I recognize—as do most people—that the boundary between moral and natural evil is grey. Indeed, I question whether "evil" is the appropriate word to describe what we call "natural evil," since evil and morality are closely linked in our minds. But these are the words typically used and so I will simply continue their usage.

Exploring Traditional Approaches to Natural Evil

Some Christians attribute natural evil to the actions of Satan and his demonic minions, who are also deemed to have free will. Positively, this view affirms that the suffering we experience is both *real* and *not* desired by God, and seeks an alternative explanation as to why a good God can't do everything we might expect *within creation*. Nevertheless, I suggest this view creates more problems than it solves. We do not know what powers angelic beings may possess and so, in one sense, this perspective simply articulates one mystery in terms of another. It also creates a dualistic framework for reality that can all too easily pit order (good) against disorder (evil). Yet as water boils we recognize there is a violent phase transition whereby relatively ordered liquid turns into disordered, chaotic steam. No one would refer to this process as evil, so we need to be mindful not to naively equate randomness and chance with demonic activity and going against God's ordering of creation. Perhaps the distinction sought for is really between predictability (divine) and unpredictability (demonic), and personalizing evil is a way to rationalize what seems like capriciousness. But even here the boundaries are grey; our world is not as black and white as this picture suggests. Quantum mechanics describes a world that has, at its heart, unpredictability at the microscopic level yet is quite predictable at a macroscopic scale (e.g., radioactive decay).[8] For these and other reasons, I don't find this dualistic way of viewing God's good creation (Gen 1:31) to be constructive or satisfying. (The role of Satan will be discussed further in the next chapter.)

There is—from our perspective—a sense of cruelty and wastefulness in the biological world. Many struggle with the seeming violence (even callousness) of a nature "red in tooth and claw," as Tennyson put it, and God's perfect goodness. In addition to predatory behavior that takes place on land, sea, and sky, we must include those things that arise *within* the bodies of creatures, namely: infections, sickness, disease, viruses, parasites, disability, genetic malformations and disorders, and—ultimately—death. In light of all this, many Christians exclaim: "This can't be the way a good God intended the natural world to be!" It is for this reason that they link such behavior and activity to the fall narrative of Genesis 3—the moral choice of Adam and Eve and the resultant "curse."

---

8. See Polkinghorne, *Science and Creation*, 34–50; Reddish, *Science and Christianity*, 92–108.

As we unpack this common understanding of this biblical story we need to begin by recognizing what is being assumed. First, it presupposes that the Creator is the omnipotent, omniscient God of perfect goodness. This is the basis of classical theism. Such a deity *would* and *could* make "the best of all possible worlds," as Leibniz claimed—which seems so plausible at first thought. After all, the psalmist tells us: "The heavens declare the glory of God; the skies proclaim the work of his hands" (Ps 19:1). And Paul reiterates that sentiment: "Ever since the creation of the world his eternal power and divine nature, invisible though they are, have been understood and seen through the things he has made" (Rom 1:20). Something wonderful—and apparently self-evident—of the Designer is to be perceived by studying his design. For instance, the regularity of nature that we admire, of day and night, and of the repetitive seasons—not just in terms of planetary motion, but of springtime and harvest—is something that we attribute to God's faithfulness and provision. This is how Christians viewed God and his creation . . . prior to Lisbon. Natural theology, where one sees signs of the Creator in creation, has too often had rose-tinted spectacles and not paid sufficient attention to the darker side of nature—as Darwin reminds us at the beginning of this chapter. What does *that* tell us about the Creator?[9] The *existence* and *extent* of natural evil have forced us to think again.[10] The added irony is that divine impassivity means that God is unmoved and impervious to the pain and suffering within creation that *we* find so troubling. Those who continue to insist on defending the honor of *this kind* of God can create a stumbling block to faith that many will trip over in the darkness of suffering. We can summarize the situation so far like this: we cannot—or dare not—blame the absolute God of classical theism, so let's blame Satan. We don't get very far if we blame Satan, so let's blame humanity. Natural evil is Adam and Eve's fault; after all, someone must be to blame!

---

9. It is therefore dangerous to extrapolate the nature or character of God by looking solely at his creation. Similarly, we do not know all about an artist by examining her painting or an author just by reading his book. What we do not know is whether the artist has her painting in pride of place or in a discarded pile, or whether the author considers his work with delight or disdain. The painter and author, who each in their own way have put something of themselves into their creations, must *reveal* what they themselves think of it. Only *they* can tell us if their work is "very good" or trash. Moreover, only they can tell us the *purpose* they intended. In regards to the creation project, then, what we need is divine revelation.

10. This is a major, I would say insurmountable, problem for the "God is in control" theodicy discussed in the next chapter.

Second, associating natural evil with Genesis 3 assumes that the Adam and Eve story is both *literal history* and intended as a *scientific* description of reality. Many struggle to separate these two aspects from the narrative because of a prior commitment to a particular understanding of the nature and purpose of Scripture, and how it should be interpreted. My own view is that the fall story is neither history nor science, but this does *not* undermine the *theological* importance of the narrative—as we will see in chapter 6. This is not the place to explore in detail my position, which is shared by many Christians, but a few comments are in order and are necessary.[11]

I take the view that the Bible's primary end is to point to *God's saving acts in history*. It is *not* a text book on science, nor is it history—as we understand history today.[12] The biblical text is prescientific; John Walton writes,

> There is not a single instance in the Old Testament of God giving scientific information that transcended the understanding of the Israelite audience. . . . Since God did not deem it necessary to communicate a different way of imagining the world to Israel but was content for them to retain the native ancient cosmic geography, we can conclude that it was not God's purpose to reveal the details of cosmic geography. . . . The shape of the earth, the nature of the sky, the locations of the sun, moon and stars, are simply not of significance, and God could communicate what he desired regardless of one's cosmic geography.[13]

Even so, for many Christians, the mention of Adam by Paul in the New Testament (e.g., Rom 5:12–21) is sufficient "proof" that Adam was a *historical*

11. See Reddish, *Science and Christianity*, 23–41, 144–67.

12. Of course the Bible contains history! However, concerning historicity, a simple comparison of the books of Kings and Chronicles will reveal the same events told from two very different perspectives. The biblical authors wrote with an agenda, (re)telling their message for the needs of their different audiences. See Enns, *The Bible Tells Me So*.

13. Walton, *Lost World of Genesis One*, 105, 16. He adds, "If [God] is consistently communicating to [the Israelite audience] in terms of their world and understanding, then why should we expect to find modern science woven between the lines? People who value the Bible do not need to make it 'speak science' to salvage its truth claims or credibility" (ibid., 105). Furthermore, David Fergusson writes, "The evidence of modern science is pretty overwhelming in terms of the age of the universe and our descent from hominid species. The biblical story must *now* be viewed as *neither* ancient history *nor* natural science, *even if this was unclear at earlier periods*. In the face of overwhelming scientific evidence, it seems unwise and unnecessary to contest this." Fergusson, *Creation*, 11, emphasis mine.

person. After all, so they claim, if you mythologize Adam you undermine (a) the saving work of Christ, (b) the notion that we are made in the image of God, and (c) the doctrine of the Fall as an explanation of suffering and evil in the world.[14] Is this really the case for (a) and (b)? I don't think so; they are both *theological* points. And implicitly in (c) is the presumption that the fall story is a *scientific* explanation (i.e., natural history), which I reject. Paul, being a man of his time, may well have believed that Adam and Eve were historical people. But so what? Is a historical Adam *essential* to Paul's *theological* argument? I, and many others, think not. After all, other New Testament writers affirm Christ as savior without the need to parallel him with Adam. Peter Enns is emphatic:

> One can believe that Paul is correct theologically and historically about the problem of sin and death and the solution that God provides in Christ without also needing to believe that his assumptions about human origins are accurate. The need for a savior does not require a historical Adam.[15]

But what about physical death? Christians, using Romans 5:12–21, often read the root cause of physical death back into the fall story. Paul's argument assumes the *reality of death* and its connection to Genesis 3 via intertestamental (or Second Temple) wisdom literature.[16] But we need not—and should not—infer from this that prior to Genesis 3 there was no cycle of birth-life-death-decay. In addition to the fossil record, we have oil in the ground whose origin requires the death of organic vegetation.[17] Christianity is not well served by those who insist God made the world with such deposits already existing in the ground! Christians who assert that death and decay only arose after a literal fall from a state of physical perfection also maintain that the laws of nature changed significantly at this time. In other words there was a real ontological change in God's created order such that—some claim—creation is no longer "good." However, most theologians emphatically reject such arguments and there is (absolutely) no such discontinuity in the scientific record. Even the proposal that God built

---

14. Ibid., 10–11.

15. Enns, *Evolution of Adam*, 143. See also Fergusson, *Creation*, 11; Polkinghorne, *Reason and Reality*, 99–104.

16. Sir 25:24; Wis 2:24; 2 Esd 3:7–22; 7:118.

17. William Hasker also states, "It is perfectly clear . . . that death, suffering and disease were not absent from the earth during all those ages: *Tyrannosaurus Rex* was not a vegetarian!" Hasker, *Triumph of God over Evil*, 104.

natural evil into the very fabric of the universe *anticipating* Adam and Eve's fateful moral decision is unsatisfying. Not only does it presuppose a particular understanding of God's relation to time (Molinism), but exegetically turns God's "very good" of Genesis 1:31 into "the best that could be done under the circumstances."[18] All these kinds of knots that need unravelling are an unnecessary consequence of a prior commitment to Scripture being infallible and inerrant concerning science and history. Instead I, like many others, concur with James Dunn regarding the *purpose* of Scripture. In his commentary on the often-quoted words of 2 Timothy 3:14–17, he states,

> The sacredness of the writings is directed to the end of "making wise for salvation"; the point of Scripture's inspiration was that the Scriptures should be beneficial for teaching and equipping the student believer for effective living as a Christian. Since this text is the most explicit biblical statement of what Scripture is *for*, the fact that it targets the purpose of Scripture so explicitly, and with a clearly delimited scope, should be given more weight, both in the doctrine and the use of Scripture. Too much time is misspent asking of Scripture what it was not designed to answer.[19]

So how should we understand the Fall? I find physicist-theologian John Polkinghorne is very insightful in this regard:

> [Adam and Eve's] turning from God did not bring biological death into the world, for that had been there for many millions of years before there were any hominids. What it did bring was what we may call "mortality," human sadness and bitterness at the inevitability of death and decay. Because our ancestors had become self-conscious they knew long beforehand that they were going to die. Because they had alienated themselves from the God whose steadfast faithfulness is the only (and sufficient) true ground for the hope of a destiny beyond death, this realization brought sorrow at the transience of human life. . . . Alienation from God brought the bitterness of mortality, but the relationship of humanity to God has been restored in the atonement (at-one-ment) brought by Jesus Christ, in whom the life of humanity and the life of divinity are both present and the broken link is mended.[20]

18. Ibid., 103–9.

19. Dunn, "2 Timothy," 853, his emphasis.

20. Polkinghorne, *Testing Scripture*, 30. Paul, in 1 Cor 15, again uses the Adam-Christ contrast and articulates the great Christian hope of ultimate resurrection and restoration. There Paul also writes of the *sting* of death being swallowed in victory; Christ's resurrection (signifying the first fruit of the final harvest) removes the fear from our

What this indicates is that the "fall" metaphor is really a falling "out" rather than a falling "down." The story is about the breakdown of *trust* and of *relationship*; between people and God, between Adam and Eve (and, later, Cain and Abel), and between themselves and the created order.[21] By not trusting the Creator, they fall out of relationship with him, resulting in separation, alienation, and disharmony.[22] The Hebrew concept of *shalom* is a restoration of peace with God, with each other, and with the created order. This is a reversal of the falling out of relationship and, for the Christian, *shalom* is ultimately achieved through the Christ-event.

In conclusion, the fall story is *not* the origin of natural evil. Indeed, it might astonish some Christians to learn that evil's origin is never identified within the Bible.[23] Evil's existence and effects are widely assumed, of course (e.g., 1 Kgs 8:46; Jer 13:23; and Ps 51), but that is hardly surprising given the *experiential* nature of suffering. Moreover, if Christian doctrine declares God's creation as *very good*, then the term "natural *evil*" is misleading.[24] The anthropocentric bias associated with natural evil is understandable, but we are left trying to explain the problem of suffering from a mistaken premise. How then might we regard the suffering we experience in the natural world? Not just the suffering that arises from defects and aging in biological processes mentioned above, but also the role of chaos and catastrophe on our geologically active, sun-heated planet that gives rise to volcanoes, earthquakes, tsunamis, hurricanes, tornadoes, floods, and famines, etc. I think the way forward is to embrace chaos and chance as morally neutral features of God's good creation, for nothing God has made is inherently evil.[25]

---

comprehension of our own mortality introduced in the fall narrative.

21. Fretheim, *God and World*, 74.

22. Note too that the final form of the text emerged in the context of the Babylonian exile. This is also alienation and an enforced expulsion from their homeland, one brought about—as they understood it—by their persistent breaking of their covenantal relationship with God. This provides added significance to Adam and Eve's expulsion from the garden.

23. See also Wright, *Evil and the Justice of God*, 45, 51, 71–74.

24. That "very good" (Gen 1:31) can also be interpreted as "aesthetically pleasing" or "fit for its intended purpose."

25. See Reddish, *Science and Christianity*, 155–67.

Natural Evil and Science

One of the central findings of many scientific disciplines (e.g., astronomy, physics, geology, and paleontology) is that the world is *old*. We are talking about 4.5 billion years for the earth and approximately 14 billion years since the big bang. Moreover, not all planets have the necessary conditions to promote and maintain life; our earth is remarkably special! For instance, we need a geologically-active planet (i.e., volcanoes and earthquakes) to sustain life. Look at our neighboring planet, Mars. It once had rivers flooding across its surface; now it is a frozen waste—in part due to the lack of plate tectonics. So we should not be quick to interpret such natural disasters, potentially catastrophic as they are for all life, as signs of God's displeasure or judgment—which is how such events would have been understood in Old Testament times.

The BBC's acclaimed *Planet Earth* television series brought natural history from all around the world, on land and in oceans, right into our living rooms. The diversity of life and habitats, together with the intricate relationships between them, was both stunningly beautiful and downright bizarre. We also witnessed "survival of the fittest" in action and the reasonableness of natural selection was overwhelmingly evident. Indeed, as mentioned earlier, it is this long-winded, evolutionary process with the seemingly wasteful dead ends that is so troublesome to many. This problem is exacerbated by the savageness of nature's finely tuned predators and the experience of fear, pain, and suffering of their prey—all for the purposes of "survival." If there were no God, we could simply say: "That is just the way the world is." But because Christians believe God is good and just, and because we believe that nonhuman life is also highly valued by God, this matter is deeply disturbing and unsatisfactory.[26]

Stepping back a moment, our developing world can be seen to arise out of the complicated interplay between chance and necessity. The "necessity" is due to the (so-called) laws of nature and the "chance" element is the way the nature's raw materials are shuffled together to create new patterns and potentialities. A conceivable outcome of this dynamic interplay would be nothing of significance. However, if the conditions are just right, then novel pseudo-stable entities could arise, not just galaxies, stars, and planetary systems, but the prerequisite complex molecules and environment necessary for life. The emergence of self-replicating living beings is a key milestone,

---

26. See Southgate, *Groaning of Creation.*

but so is sufficient stability to enable—over time—the development of life with increasing diversity, complexity, and even self-consciousness.

In addition to this subtle relationship between randomness and regularity, the environment in which animal and plant life is evolving is also changing. Moreover, our planet's biological systems are not "closed" to the outside, but are continually receiving and generating energy. If the changes in the surrounding conditions (e.g., temperature, radiation input, localized chemical composition and concentrations, etc.) alter sufficiently, the opportunity for a certain kind of evolutionary change may be lost. This means that in addition to chance and necessity there is *history*. And history, because of the arrow of time, is not repeatable. Consequently, evolutionary development involves unpredictability and irreversibility.[27] This process inevitably results in blind alleys, as well as major extinctions—like the dinosaurs—due to dramatic changes in the environment, such as catastrophic meteor impacts and ice ages. Time's directionality means that a particular progression cannot be reversed and some more fruitful direction explored. However, the mere fact that we are here demonstrates that not all chance is destructive. Rather this exploratory process creates an openness to original emergent possibilities, some of which can—evidently—also be positive.

Obviously the Christian adds an important layer of meaning to the above description since *God* is the Creator and Sustainer of the universe! John Polkinghorne writes,

> In his great act of creation . . . God allows the physical world to be itself, not in . . . opposition to him, but in that independence which is Love's gift of freedom to the one beloved. The world is endowed in its fundamental constitution with an *anthropic* potentiality which makes it capable of fruitful evolution.[28]

Biochemist-theologian Arthur Peacocke speaks of natural processes displaying certain tendencies, which are strong enough to be termed *propensities*, for an increase in complexity and organization within living systems, even to the point of the emergence of consciousness and self-awareness.[29]

---

27. Barbour, *Religion and Science*, 238.

28. Polkinghorne, *Science and Providence*, 77, emphasis mine. He adds, "The exploration and realization of that potentiality is achieved by the universe through the continual interplay of chance and necessity within its unfolding process. The cosmos is given the opportunity to be itself."

29. Peacocke, *Theology for a Scientific Age*, 156. He also writes, "If all were governed by rigid law, a repetitive and uncreative order would prevail: if chance alone ruled, no forms, patterns or organizations would persist long enough for them to have any identity

For the Christian, such propensities will obviously be interpreted as built in to the fabric of the cosmos and *intended* by God. In this sense the dice is loaded or biased so that over time God's creation explores such emergent possibilities through the complex interplay of chance and necessity (i.e., the lawlike framework that constrains the possibilities). Consequently, evolutionary development is creative and can produce "good" outcomes, such as healthy conscious beings and a diverse variety of plant and animal life.[30] Nevertheless, it is also an untidy process and inevitably results in physical "evils," such as disease, genetic deformities, and death, along with a great deal of suffering.[31] It seems we cannot have one without the other. John Polkinghorne concludes,

> [We live in] a world of orderliness but not of clockwork regularity, of potentiality without predictability, endowed with an assurance of development but with a certain openness as to its actual form. It is inevitably a world with ragged edges, where order and disorder interlace each other and where the exploration of possibility by chance will lead not only to the evolution of systems of increasing complexity, endowed with new possibilities, but also to the evolution of systems imperfectly formed and malfunctioning.[32]

For Polkinghorne, the world is "endowed with an *assurance* of development" because *God* designed the system of law and chance.[33] Yet God only designs the general system; the specific details are *not* explicit expressions of God's will. Elsewhere Polkinghorne adds: "God no more expressly wills the growth of a cancer than he expressly wills the act of a murderer. . . . He

---

or real existence and the universe could never be a cosmos and susceptible to rational enquiry. It is the combination of the two which makes possible an ordered universe capable of developing within itself new modes of existence. *The interplay of chance and law is creative*" (ibid., 65, his emphasis).

30. Incidentally, a geologically "dead" planet, like Mars, or one without a strong magnetosphere to protect it from energetic solar radiation, has little prospect for harboring the kind of life we find on Earth.

31. Arthur Peacocke writes, "*Pain and suffering*, on the one hand, and *consciousness of pleasure and well-being*, on the other, *are emergents* in the world. The presence of the latter never causes any surprise (why not?) and it is the presence of the former which . . . is usually taken to constitute a problem for belief in a creating God." Peacocke, *Theology for a Scientific Age*, 68, his emphasis.

32. Polkinghorne, *Science and Creation*, 49.

33. Arthur Peacocke makes exactly the same point: "*God is the ultimate ground and source for both law ('necessity') and chance.*" Peacocke, *Theology for a Scientific Age*, 119, his emphasis.

is not the puppet master of either men or matter."[34] This point needs emphasizing for the *individual*: this theodicy does *not* require us to think that a person's experience of suffering (arising from natural physical, chemical, and biological processes) is either good, or illusionary, or deliberately planned by God.[35] While God does not predestine every event, nevertheless *this is the kind of world* that God freely chose to make. In an analogous way to God having created humans with genuine free will, God has similarly created the world with relative autonomy and provides the space for these processes to develop freely. Paralleling Alvin Plantinga's free will defense, Polkinghorne calls this description the "free process defense."[36] He adds: "The free will and free process defenses are two sides of one coin, the cost of a world given independence through the loving gift of its Creator."[37]

In summary, our dynamic world is not risk free for humans. In addition to regularity, God has made a world with a significant element of chaos and disharmony that is an integral and essential part of a world that is in the process of "becoming." Volcanoes are needed to replenish our atmosphere in order to sustain life; this requires a planet with an active geology. The earth has plate tectonics with earthquakes and tsunamis. Our sun-heated atmosphere gives rise to the water cycle and sustains life; but it also produces hurricanes, tornadoes, and cyclones. These messy, disorderly

34. Polkinghorne, *Science and Providence*, 78. See also Polkinghorne, *Exploring Reality*, 143–46.

35. That said, this view of creation does provide foundational support for John Hick's "soul-making" theodicy discussed in the next chapter. But it falls short of claiming the need for moral progress *is the divine reason* for the presence of physical suffering in the world. The term *theodicy*, discussed further in the next chapter, literally means "justifying God" in view of the existence of evil.

36. Ibid., 143, and Polkinghorne, *Science and Providence*, 77. Alvin Plantinga's free will defense will be discussed in the next chapter. Strictly speaking, a "defense" is not a "theodicy." All a defense needs to show, in this context, is that it is logically *possible* for a good and powerful God to create a world in which natural evil can arise and still be consistent with his character. A theodicy ("defending God") is a step further; it believes the propositions are not merely *possible*, but *plausible*, even *probable*. Christians who also embrace a scientific worldview are really wrestling with theodicy because we accept the well-established findings of science as provisionally "true" (i.e., critical realism), together with our faith in God's character and capabilities. Consequently, I take Polkinghorne's "free process defense" to be a "theodicy." Two other similar theodicies are (a) Southgate's "only way" theodicy, i.e., "an evolving creation was the *only way* in which God could give rise to the sort of beauty, diversity, sentience, and sophistication of creatures that the biosphere now contains" (*Groaning of Creation*, 16, emphasis mine; see also 47–48); and (b) Hasker's "natural-order theodicy" (see Hasker, *Triumph of God over Evil*, 122–46).

37. Polkinghorne, *Exploring Reality*, 144.

natural disasters have a role to play in our ever-changing world. Order and chaos are inseparable; physical violence and the birth-life-death-decay cycle are features of God's *good* world. And we acknowledge that these—and other—events also have the capacity to bring pain and suffering to both human and nonhuman life. God's good world is *untamed*, but God isn't tame either—and we need to be mindful of the tendency within theodicies to domesticate God.[38]

Conclusion

Is this of *any* comfort to a person who is suffering, or to someone—like me—whose wife died from cancer at a young age? What should be apparent is that all theodicies are of limited value, but especially those that pertain to impersonal processes that constitute what we call "natural evil." It is of no comfort to a sufferer to say "Satan is behind this disease," or, "Your cancer is a consequence of Adam and Eve's decision," or, "That earthquake is simply a feature of God's untamed world." At least all three of these theodicies don't blame God directly! However insightful these natural evil theodicies may be—and I obviously prefer the latter—they are not meant to be a *personal* explanation for a *particular* woe, and so we should not expect too much from them. As William Hasker writes,

> [Such theodicies], if accepted, vindicate God's wisdom and goodness as seen in the general order of creation; [they do] not speak of God's particular concern for individual human beings. But God's love for individuals is absolutely crucial for Christian faith; it is not something that should conceivably be given up.[39]

And Christopher Southgate concludes,

> All theodicies that engage with real situations rather than philosophical abstractions, and endeavour to give an account of the God of the Christian Scriptures, arise out of protest and end in mystery. Theodicies never "work," in the sense of solving the problem of suffering in the world. But if a theodicy . . . stirs others to greater compassion for creaturely pain, to deeper prayer, and to

---

38. Hasker, *Triumph of God over Evil*, 146. Note too that C. S. Lewis's Aslan, the lion of Narnia, is not tame, but he is good.

39. Ibid., 145. Note: William Hasker's quote was originally with reference to his "natural-order theodicy." I have broadened his conclusion to include other theodicies that also pertain to natural evil.

partnering, in however small a way, [with] the loving and merciful purposes of God, then it has done all that can be hoped of it.[40]

There is an obvious *cost* to this creation, one that all life capable of pain and suffering knows firsthand. Given the scale of evil, both moral and natural, a Christian cannot help but wonder if the cost is ultimately justified. But that is not where the matter ends because the Creator is neither the unmoved Mover of classical theism, nor the absentee Landlord of deism. God's initial and continuing acts of creation are *not* the last word on divine action. Christians believe the Trinitarian God has also chosen to be intimately and incessantly involved in history, and, I believe, to co-suffer with creation. The incarnation demonstrates that divine participation is not from a distance, and Father, Son, and Spirit *all* experience suffering as Jesus absorbs the world's evil on the cross. John Polkinghorne concludes:

> One might dare to say that the burden of existential anguish at the suffering of the world is not borne by creatures alone, but their Creator shares the load, thereby enabling its ultimate redemption. . . . The Christian God is the crucified God, not a compassionate spectator from the outside but truly a fellow sufferer who understands creatures' pain from the inside. Only at this most profound level can theology begin truly to engage in the problem of evil and suffering of this world.[41]

And Gregory Boyd adds,

> Christ's incarnation, death and resurrection reveal that though God is not culpable for the evil in the world, he nevertheless takes responsibility for it. And in taking responsibility for evil, he overcomes it. On the cross God suffers at the hands of evil. In this suffering and through his resurrection he destroys evil in principle. Through the cross and resurrection God unequivocally displays his loving character and establishes his loving purposes for the world despite its evil resistance. He thereby demonstrates that evil is not something he wills *into* existence: it's something he wills *out of* existence.[42]

Now *that's* encouragement for the sufferer! But before we can develop this crucial theme further, one that is unique to Christianity, we need first to consider to the problem of moral evil.

40. Southgate, *Groaning of Creation*, 132–33.
41. Polkinghorne, *Exploring Reality*, 146.
42. Boyd, *Is God to Blame?*, 91, his emphasis.

5

Does God Always Get What God Wants?

The line dividing good and evil cuts through the heart of every human being.

—ALEKSANDR SOLZHENITSYN

Introduction

Richard Rice, in *Suffering and the Search for Meaning*, reminds us that suffering is *personal*: "When pain *appears* in the world, I face the problem of evil; when pain and loss *invade* my world, I face the problem of suffering."[1] The enduring "problem of evil" can all too easily become a sterile debating topic between armchair theologians and philosophers, leaving those *experiencing* suffering confused and uncomforted. Good theology, however, is not purely academic, but informed by experience and is both relevant and applicable to *real* life.[2] Nevertheless, because reality is complex, we should not expect the outcomes of theological deliberations to be simple. If they were, we would dismiss those conclusions as

---

1. Rice, *Suffering and the Search for Meaning*, 153, his emphasis. I acknowledge that the material in his excellent and accessible book provided the basis of this chapter.

2. Douglas John Hall writes, "*Doctrine has always to be submitted to the test of life. Doctrine must serve life, not life doctrine.*" Hall, *Cross in Our Context*, 28, his emphasis.

trivializing the persistence of evil and the myriad of issues that permeate and exacerbate our experience of suffering.

In this chapter we will explore a number of popular theodicies. The word *theodicy*, introduced by Leibniz in 1710, is an offensive and impious word to some because it literally means "justifying God," i.e., defending God in light of the existence of evil. It is true that theodicies tend to claim too much if they imply knowing with confidence the mind of God, or if they claim to give a definitive answer to the question, "Why?" That is *not* the intent here. Indeed, my starting point is to say evil can *never* be justified. Moreover, no religious arguments *should* attempt to justify God in connection with abuse, rape, torture, ethnic "cleansing," etc.[3] Nevertheless, it is legitimate for a skeptic to ask of a Christian how he/she understands God's character and action given the reality of suffering and evil. A response *is* required, even if it is only tentative. However, the theological frameworks we articulate are for our benefit—not God's—and therefore need not be equated with *defending* God.[4]

Christians affirm that God is both good and powerful. As we saw in chapter 2, a qualified understanding of God's power is critical. However, most people's default assumption is that God is omnipotent. That being the case, and given the presence of horrendous evils in the world, the simple question they understandably ask is: "Why doesn't God *use* his power?" Douglas John Hall writes,

> What such persons seem not to grasp, or even entertain, is that gods who prevent evil and set everything to rights can only do so by overruling the behavior of that one creature that creates more havoc than any other: ourselves. Ironically, those who most complain of God's failure to act godlike, that is, to exercise unmitigated power, are the very ones who are most affronted by any curtailment of their own freedom. They want the world to be what they want the world to be, and the only god they can abide is one whose will coincides perfectly with their own.[5]

If we are honest with ourselves, he has a valid point! Moreover, we approach the problem of suffering assuming a certain kind of God, *usually the deity of classical theism*. This is very much the case in theodicy, as we saw in the previous chapter—and will see again here.

3. See also Hasker, *Triumph of God over Evil*, 10.

4. For further discussion of these sensibilities, see ibid., 120–22.

5. Hall, *Cross in Our Context*, 87.

The crucible of suffering causes us to examine *the kind of God we be-lieve in* and *the nature of the world God made*. The previous three chapters address those two foundational aspects and remind us that the Trinity is at the heart of the Christian tradition. Ironically, you should note that there is no explicit mention of Father, Son, and Spirit in this chapter. This reflects the *philosophical* nature of theodicy, and a Christian will want to see coher-ence with the character, purposes, and action of God depicted here with that arising from *theological* reflection. The use of reason is very important, but it is only one aspect of theology—the others being Scripture, church tradition, and experience (or context). I believe, however, that our theo-logical framework must start with the Trinity and work outward into all areas of theology and the life of the church, including our understanding of suffering. The following chapters will develop this theme further, but it is toward theodicy and moral evil that we turn first.

"God Is in Control"

A person came up to me at my wife's funeral to offer me comfort and en-couragement using the well-worn phrase: "God is in control." I knew it was kindly meant and so I did not take offense. I smiled politely and said nothing; I had heard this phrase many times before. For many Christians "God is in control" is central to their theological outlook. God has not only *planned* all of history (in every detail) but—either directly or indirectly—*brings about* his plans. Logically, it then follows that "God's plan is perfect" for "God never makes mistakes." Inescapably, this means that God is the author of both good *and* evil, since God is absolutely sovereign.

Consider the inspiring biblical story of Joseph whose jealous and vin-dictive brothers sold him into slavery in Egypt, and who was later wrong-fully imprisoned. He eventually rose to power and influence in the royal court. His actions saved many people from famine, including his own fam-ily. As Joseph later forgives and reconciles with his fearful brothers, he says to them: "Even though you intended to do harm to me, God intended it for good" (Gen 50:20). The author, like many Old Testament writers, saw Joseph's heroic journey from victim to savior as *divinely purposed* from be-ginning to end.

In 1967 Joni Eareckson Tada had a diving accident as a teenager that tragically left her a quadriplegic. Her life story of courage and faith has inspired millions, including me.[6] Her understanding of God's role in suffering is, perhaps, startling:

> When God *allows* something, he is acting *deliberately*—he is *decreeing* that event. . . . Unless the Bible is wrong, *nothing* happens outside of God's decree. Nothing good, nothing bad, nothing pleasant, nothing tragic . . . We may not fathom God's reasons . . . we may love him for it, we may hate him for it. But in simple language, God runs the world. . . . Either God rules, or Satan sets the world's agenda and God is limited to reacting. In which case, the Almighty would become Satan's clean-up boy.[7]

In this view, if God didn't control evil, the result would be evil uncontrollable. And if, instead of deliberately planning them, God merely reacts to suffering after they occur or patches them up, then our sufferings would have no real meaning.[8] While the intent behind these statements is, no doubt, to give glory and honor to God, it nevertheless paints a picture of an all-or-nothing deity who must *necessarily* be in absolute control. Nevertheless, one can legitimately ask: "Is it categorically true that God *must* be a micromanager, *else* he is 'Satan's clean-up boy'?"

Millions have read Rick Warren's *The Purpose Driven Life* and have incorporated the thinking within his best-selling book into their lives. There Warren states, "God has a purpose behind every problem."[9] He continues,

> None of your problems could happen without God's permission. Everything that happens to a child of God is *Father-filtered*, and he intends to use it for good even when Satan and others mean it for bad. Because God is sovereignly in control, accidents are just incidents in God's good plan for you. Because every day of your life was written on God's calendar before you were born, *everything* that happens to you has spiritual significance.[10]

---

6. Tada, *Joni*.

7. Tada and Estes, *When God Weeps*, 82, 76, 84, emphasis mine.

8. Rice, *Suffering and the Search for Meaning*, 28–30.

9. Warren, *Purpose Driven Life*, 193.

10. Ibid., 194–95, his emphasis. In my view, God "permitting" or "allowing" suffering and "causing" it (albeit indirectly) is, in essence, the same thing. I appreciate one can argue for subtle nuanced differences between them—not least, as divine "permission" can, in principle, be contrasted to divine "prevention" and "intervention." However, both words entail a strong view of divine sovereignty and power. Thomas Jay Oord puts it this way: "A God worthy of our worship cannot be Someone who *causes, supports,* or *allows* genuine evil." Oord, *Uncontrolling Love of God*, 68, emphasis mine.

Timothy Keller says the same thing:

> Everything that happens fits in accord with, in harmony with, God's plan (Eph 1:11). This means God's plan includes "little things." . . . Even the flip of the coin is part of his plan (Prov 16:33). Ultimately, there are no accidents. His plan also includes bad things. . . . Suffering then is not outside of God's plan but a part of it.[11]

While I have respect for Rick Warren and Tim Keller, I am deeply uncomfortable with the view that suffering is an integral part of God's *personalized* plan for us. In fact, I think it's wrong. Again, this view emphasizes God's absolute sovereignty, together with unqualified divine attributes of omniscience and omnipotence. The mystery of suffering is firmly located in the mind of God, whose ways are not our ways (Isa 55:8–9). Since God is all-wise, finite human beings are simply to trust in God's wisdom and perfect plan for us. There *are* good reasons for all of life's sufferings, we are told, it is just that they are unknowable to us in this life.

A similar viewpoint is expressed movingly in an anonymous poem, "My Life Is but a Weaving," popularized by Corrie ten Boom (1892–1983):[12]

> My Life is but a weaving
> between my Lord and me;
> I cannot choose the colors
> He worketh steadily.
> Oft times He weaveth sorrow
> And I, in foolish pride,
> Forget He sees the upper,
> And I the underside.
> Not til the loom is silent
> And the shuttles cease to fly,

---

11. Keller, *Walking with God*, 141. Elsewhere Timothy Keller writes, "Though [not] grateful for the tragedies themselves, they would not trade the insight, character and strength they had gotten from them for anything. With time and perspective most of us can see good reasons for at least *some* of the tragedy and pain that occurs in life. Why couldn't it be possible that, from God's vantage point, there are good reasons for all of them?" Keller, *Reason for God*, 25, his emphasis. Ravi Zacharias and Vince Vitale concur; see Zacharias and Vitale, *Why Suffering?*, 197.

12. While living in occupied Holland during the Second World War, Corrie and her family helped Jews escape the Holocaust. Corrie was arrested in February 1944 and eventually sent to Ravensbrück concentration camp along with her sister, Betsie, who later died there. Her amazing story is told in *The Hiding Place*, first published in 1971. This tapestry imagery is also described in Thornton Wilder's novel *The Eighth Day*; cited in Kushner, *When Bad Things Happen*, 17–18.

Shall God unroll the canvas
And explain the reason why.
The dark threads are as needful
In the Weaver's skillful hand,
As the threads of gold and silver
In the pattern He has planned.
He knows, He loves, He cares,
Nothing this truth can dim.
He gives His very best to those
Who leave the choice with Him.

This well-known picture of a tapestry being woven by the Master Weaver is meant to be comforting—and many find it so. It speaks of God's plan, power, and purpose in all the events of an individual's life, including the dark threads of sorrow. We are to be reassured that, although we only see the messy underside of life's tapestry, God is weaving something beautiful. We might not understand how suffering could be part of God's "good plan" for us, but one day we will. Consequently, the answer to the question, "Does God always get what God wants?" is, "Indeed, yes."

There are positive things one can appreciate in this theodicy. For example, we do not need to waste time and energy with self-recrimination or regret. Since our life's experiences are all divinely planned and for our best, we need not be troubled by "What if?" questions. This viewpoint also appeals to our desire for order and meaning since it totally rejects that *anything* happens "by chance." On that point, R. C. Sproul is adamant:

> The mere existence of chance is enough to rip God from his cosmic throne. . . . If [chance] exists as a mere impotent, humble servant, it leaves God not only out of date, but out of a job. If chance exists in its frailest possible form, God is finished. . . . If chance exists in any size, shape, or form, God cannot exist. The two are mutually exclusive. If chance existed, it would destroy God's sovereignty.[13]

Note that there is assumed to be only two options in this way of thinking: meticulous control of every last detail *or* total chance, randomness, and chaos. This describes a digital, black-and-white world ruled by order and certainty; divine sovereignty is equated with total control.

Without doubt one can find biblical verses to lend support this view, particularly in the Old Testament.[14] But this is not a compelling argument

13. Sproul, *Not a Chance*, 3.

14. For example, Isa 46:9–11; Ps 115:3; Prov 16; 19:21. It has also been a persistent

in itself as biblical cases can be made for all the theodicies presented in this chapter. And, as we have seen, the Christian doctrine of God is bigger than simply quoting a selection of Bible verses. On reflection, it is apparent that this portrayal of the Divine is more in keeping with the imperial God of classical theism than that of the social Trinity. That should give pause for thought. The strong support this view holds in some Christian traditions suggests that contemporary Trinitarian theology has still much more to do in influencing the life of the church.

There are other serious criticisms of the "God is in control" theodicy. There continues to be a *massive* amount of suffering in the world. This arises both from human agency and through natural disasters, which we considered in the previous chapter. We can list but a few here: the terror attacks on 9/11, followed by other major attacks in, for example, London, Istanbul, Paris, Nice, Baghdad, and Madrid; the Syrian civil war and the Mediterranean refugee crisis; the AIDS, Zika, and Ebola viruses; major natural disasters, like hurricane Katrina, the Haiti earthquake, and the Indian Ocean tsunami.[15] One can go back to two major World Wars: the Holocaust, Hiroshima and Nagasaki, as well as all the more recent conflicts. The list goes on and on, both around the globe and throughout history. Is all this suffering *really* necessary? Moreover, are we really saying God *planned* and "*decreed*" them all? Frankly, this is not credible to the thinking Christian, let alone to someone inquiring about the faith.

In addition to the above strong theological reservations, I have major pastoral concerns on the emotive, high-stakes rhetoric used and the way it is wrapped in unquestionable biblical authority. I think this can trap Christians wrestling with doubts, disappointment, or anger in light of their personal suffering. It is hard to draw comfort from the psalmist who says, "God is our refuge and strength, a very present help in trouble" (Ps 46:1) if, in fact, God planned and executed it! This can result in bitterness toward God and the inability to forgive—let alone love—him. Whatever evils *others* may have done, they hold *God* accountable since the ultimate explanation lies in the sovereign will of God. This can be confusing for the Christian too. Should I pray for God to heal my wife from cancer? However, it would obviously make no sense to pray for God's healing if I believed God sent it!

---

feature within church history; Protestants associate predestination with Calvinism.

15. Hurricanes occur annually and 2017 had a notable series of devastating storms (Harvey, Irma, and Maria). Around the same time, Mexico was experiencing deadly, major earthquakes.

While some find hope and peace in simply trusting this all-controlling God, others see such a God as tyrannical and fear-inducing, rather than one worthy of devotion. Moreover, if people are told *definitively* that God is this kind of deity and that he relates with his creation in this specific way, then this can lead to a "take-it-or-leave-it" version of Christianity. This is a tragic message to convey to those who are suffering. To those in this position I say, "Read on, and discover other God-honoring alternatives."[16]

Nevertheless, I genuinely respect people—like Joni and Corrie ten Boom—who hold this faith position, *if* they have discovered this view to be true *for themselves* in the face of suffering. One can only admire their courageous faith. I suggest, however, that to present this perspective *to another* (i.e., as corresponding to the divine meaning or purpose behind suffering) is in the same category of blunder as Job's well-meaning friends. I don't think God's honor is enhanced by insisting on this "God is in control" theodicy. Rather, it is seriously undermined. Moreover, this view can gravely damage another's faith. Ironically, the one thing Job's famed "comforters" got right was to first sit in silence with him for a week and so identify with his suffering (Job 2:11–13). It is also worth pointing out that while Job's friends upheld the traditional wisdom of the Old Testament, their views were apparently *not* God's views on the matter (Job 42:7–9)!

The critical theological question is simply: "Is suffering *inside* or *outside* of God's specific will?" If—following Keller—our response is "inside" then it would seem that the appropriate response is to passively accept it and seek God's help to endure it. To fight against suffering is, in a sense, to resist God's will. Frankly, I find this bizarre. After all, Jesus' response to disease was to heal it! On the other hand, if suffering is "outside" of God's *specific* will then we are not only free to oppose suffering, but we can be assured that in so doing the Trinitarian God is on our side. As Rice says, "We have every right to resent it, resist it, relieve it, and try and eliminate it."[17] Consequently, the answer to the question, "Does God always get what God wants?" is, "Definitely not."

The Free Will Defense

The "God is in control" answer to the problem of suffering arises primarily from theology and is based on a particular understanding of Scripture.

16. See also Boyd, *Is God to Blame?*
17. Rice, *Suffering and the Search for Meaning*, 48.

There are alternative responses which also incorporate insights from philosophy and science. Foundational to all arguments is the nature of free will. One form is referred to as *libertarian*. This means that (at least some of) the decisions we make are genuinely free, implying that we are really able to make meaningful choices. In other words, we have real options and can act intentionally. This also means that, until we make this choice, not even God can know *exactly* what we will choose.[18] The second form is called *compatibilist* which claims that humankind's moral responsibility is nevertheless compatible with God being sovereignly in control of all events.[19] In other words, we are free even though all are future actions are already certain. Can we know what kind of free will we possess—compatibilist or libertarian? Obviously not. I will be up-front here, I—like many—struggle to see how human freedom can be consistent with theological determinism and therefore I believe we possess libertarian free will. Clearly, our assumptions concerning the nature of free will have important theological consequences.

The traditional conundrum of the problem of evil can be articulated in this way:

1. A perfectly good God would *want* to eliminate evil;

2. An all-powerful God would be *able* to eliminate it;

3. Yet evil exists.[20]

Since (3) is evidently true, which premise do we question: (1) or (2)—or both? While some might say the first (God is not perfectly good), most prefer to query the second premise (God is not all-powerful). Others would say this means God does not exist. We have already explored the

18. Although it is not unreasonable to assume God knows every *possible* outcome prior to our decision. God's omniscience—like his omnipotence—is therefore qualified. In addition, much depends on how one views God's relationship with *time*. This complex topic has been accessibly summarized in Evans and Manis, *Philosophy of Religion*, 42–52; Peterson et al., *Reason and Religious Belief*, 176–87; Reddish, *Science and Christianity*, 115–24.

19. Since God determines or causes all things (either directly or indirectly), then he knows all things—from the very beginning—including all the outcomes of the decisions we make. Nevertheless, God holds *us* accountable for choices we make.

20. This formulation of the problem of evil is attributed to the Greek philosopher Epicurus (341–270 BCE). The Scottish skeptic David Hume restates the matter in his *Dialogues concerning Natural Religion* (1779): "Is [God] willing to prevent evil, but not able? Then is he impotent. Is he able, but not willing? Then is he malevolent. Is he both able and willing? Whence then is evil?" Cited in Hasker, *Triumph of God over Evil*, 55.

issue of God's omnipotence in chapter 2. There we acknowledged that God is bound by logic, that God's omnipotence means God can do anything that *for God* is *logically* possible and that does not involve a contradiction. But philosophers widely recognize that Alvin Plantinga's free will defense means that the second statement is still not necessarily true, as previously assumed.[21] A "defense" is not a "theodicy," rather it demonstrates the *logical* consistency between God's existence and the presence of evil in the world. It should therefore not be confused with a theodicy's attempt to "justify God."[22] Plantinga's success is remarkable, as many see the problem of evil as the atheist's trump card to prove the nonexistence of God.

God has created agents with genuine (libertarian) free will and those creatures have the real capability to make important choices. Some of those decisions will either align with or go against the desires of the Creator. God chose to give that freedom, and once God had made such creatures he could not then "uncreate" them and still be consistent with his character.[23] Why would God make such creatures? Their freedom represents such a huge risk! The traditional theological response is *out of love*; the Trinity's mutual love overflows into creative acts. Moreover, God desires to have a relationship with those creatures having free will, and they have the unique capability to *respond* to that love—a love that is initiated by God (1 John 4:19). They also have the freedom to reject God's offer of intimacy. It is therefore no accident that the biblical God is likened to a good parent.[24] Mutual love requires authentic freedom. A reciprocal response to God's self-giving love cannot be coerced—else it would not arise from genuine love. In the same way, faith requires the liberty to doubt. God cannot determine or program either love or faith without destroying the very meaning of those terms; indeed, destroy our very humanity.

21. See Plantinga, *God, Evil and Freedom*. To my knowledge, no philosopher has found a way to successfully refute the basic logic in the free will defense. For further details, see Hasker, *Triumph of God over Evil*, 63; Rice, *Suffering and the Search for Meaning*, 43–50.

22. I appreciate that how I use Alvin Plantinga's defense, i.e., merging theology with philosophy, could be argued as doing precisely that! See Hasker, *Triumph of God over Evil*, 20–21; 57–65. Note that showing the argument is logically coherent does not prove the truth of the propositions themselves.

23. Indeed, in the biblical story of Noah, God is portrayed as deeply troubled and as regretting making humankind because of their wickedness (Gen 6:5–7). We will consider Noah again in chapter 6.

24. For example: Ps 103:13; Isa 66:13; Eph 3:14–15.

The free will defense continues: God, in creating *this kind* of world, gave us genuine freedom. That being the case, God cannot be held responsible for how we use that freedom. Putting it more formally: "God is responsible for the *possibility* of evil, but not for the *actuality* of evil."[25] Moral evil—the evils that arise from the choices we freely make—is therefore a consequence of humankind's abuse of freedom. Such evil acts do not originate with God and are not intended by God. Moreover, as mentioned earlier, God cannot—or does not—unilaterally override free will without being inconsistent with his character.[26]

Two things follow from this argument. First, this frees us from blaming God directly for the suffering that others inflict on us. Sadly, the negative effects of decisions that go against the Creator's desires can be perpetuated for generations. We see this from the patterns of abuse within family systems to the lingering effects of pollution in nature. Second, God's assumed omnipotence—premise 2—now needs to be qualified to incorporate the acts of agents with free will. Events in this world are determined by God *and* creatures, and not by God alone. For God's desires to be realized therefore *requires* the cooperation of creatures with free will.[27] This then is an argument against the "God" of classical theism, but *not* the suffering Trinitarian God. It opens up new avenues for exploring the age-old problem of suffering; we will now consider some of them.[28]

25. Rice, *Suffering and the Search for Meaning*, 47, his emphasis.

26. The subtle, though important, issue of "cannot" or "does not" is discussed in Oord, *Uncontrolling Love of God*. Briefly, "does not" is a matter of divine self-restraint; "cannot" implies God is literally unable to do so. The theological origin of both is in our understanding of the nature of divine love. I favor the divine self-restraint argument. The matter of "cannot" will be referred to again in the "even God can't do everything" theodicy.

27. This fatally undermines Leibniz's "best possible" world theodicy, discussed in the previous chapter. If creatures with free will fail to cooperate with God, then the best possible world will not exist, despite God's best efforts. See Hasker, *Triumph of God over Evil*, 77–82.

28. I fully appreciate that the philosophical success of the free will defense is of little comfort to the victims of injustice and oppression delivered by their fellow human beings. What this does suggest, however, is the high value—and responsibility—that God places on human free will. In light of that, it is no surprise that accountability before God for how we use our free will, both individually and collectively, is a theme that runs throughout Scripture.

"What Does Not Kill You Makes You Stronger"

Those familiar words are also the (extended) title of the catchy hit song by Kelly Clarkson. As with many songs with dubious lyrics that are given excessive air time, they can become annoying! But the phrase graphically illustrates the "no pain, no gain" theodicy to the problem of suffering. As we will see, at its heart is the claim that suffering is a normal, divinely-purposed, part of life, and it is *how* we respond to it that really matters. It places a positive spin on adversity by focusing the attention on the beneficial outcome—the "gain."

It is worth affirming, at the outset, that suffering has the *potential* to teach us a great deal. Our most painful experiences can be occasions for growth and development. This sentiment is echoed by the poet Robert Browning Hamilton:

> I walked a mile with Pleasure.
> She chattered all the way,
> But left me none the wiser
> For all she had to say.
>
> I walked a mile with Sorrow,
> And ne'er a word said she;
> But, oh, the things I learned from her
> When Sorrow walked with me!

The idea that personal growth is learned along the unwanted path of pain is also to be found in the Bible. The profound story of the righteous Job's suffering can be seen in this light. And in the New Testament, Paul writes,

> But we also boast in our sufferings, knowing that suffering produces endurance, and endurance produces character, and character produces hope, and hope does not disappoint us, because God's love has been poured into our hearts through the Holy Spirit that has been given to us.[29]

This is, I suggest, not to perversely "boast *because of* our sufferings" or glory in affliction, rather Paul is encouraging his readers to be persistent *in* suffering and to remind us that our Christian hope overcomes our present dismay.[30] It is not a call to embrace stoicism or shallow optimism; nor is

---

29. Rom 5:3–5.

30. There may be another qualification to consider too, namely suffering "for the sake of the gospel," e.g., Matt 5:11–12; Mark 8:34–35; 2 Tim 1:8.

it passive or fatalistic. Rather, it is encouragement for the journey through the wilderness toward the promised land.[31] It is a call for hope-filled endurance, based on the fact that Jesus led the way in this regard, and because we have the life-giving Spirit with us as we travel.

We have all been inspired by contemporary stories of people who have been transformed by suffering rather than being obliterated by it. For example, we have heard of incredible expressions of forgiveness toward, say, the killer of a loved one.[32] Or of parents turning their personal tragedy into something beneficial for others, thereby creating a meaning-making legacy for their child. As profoundly moving and important though such examples undoubtedly are, pain and suffering also have the potential to destroy us. Not just physically, but to kill our spirit—leading to suicide—and to do irreparable damage to our trust in God and in humankind. We cannot, and should not, overlook this obvious fact.

The "no pain, no gain" approach considers suffering as an *inevitable* part of the human maturation process. There is no route to moral maturity without suffering, so the argument goes. It takes Paul's view of "character development as a consequence of suffering" and turns it on its head: the need for moral progress *is the reason* for the presence of suffering in the world. John Hick is one modern proponent of this view, which was developed from an idea mentioned by Irenaeus of Lyons (ca. 130–202). Much of Western theology is strongly influenced by St. Augustine; in this context, it is the traditional doctrine of original sin that is rejected. The story of the humanity's "fall" in Genesis 3 does not fit in with evolutionary development. For Hick, indeed for many, the Fall is a story and not factual history.[33] Hick argues that we don't start off in a state of perfection and fall from grace, rather the opposite: we begin imperfect and immature. It

31. Wright, "Letter to the Romans," 516–17. See also 1 Cor 10:13.

32. For example, recall the prompt outpouring of forgiveness from the local Amish community to the family of the killer when, on October 2, 2006, a gunman entered a one-room Amish school in Nickel Mines, Pennsylvania, and killed five girls and critically wounded others before killing himself. (For further details see http://amishgrace.com.) Recall too the remarkable story of Gordon Wilson, whose daughter, Marie, was killed by an IRA bomb during Enniskillen's Remembrance Day parade in 1987; he himself was injured in the blast. Shortly after watching her die, he spoke emotionally on the BBC News, saying, "I bear no ill will. I bear no grudge." He publicly forgave the IRA and urged for there to be no reprisals. He went on to be an influential peace campaigner in Northern Ireland, working tirelessly for forgiveness and reconciliation.

33. I disagree with Hick as to the theological significance of the fall story. Nevertheless, I agree it is not literal history.

is through hardships that we mature morally and develop character. Indeed, he also maintains that this struggle is actually what God intended, and hence why—of necessity—this is not a risk-free world. Patience and persistence would not develop if everything came easily to us. Our lives then, according to this view, are on a trajectory toward eventual perfection at the eschaton.

In the standard free will defense, God desires that we *remain* loyal to him—hence there is an attachment to a traditional view of humanity's "fall," whether taken literally or nonliterally. It is quite the opposite in Hick's "vale of soul-making" perspective; God desires that we *become* loyal to him.[34] Both views require genuine (libertarian) free will. Both agree God does not plan or approve of our mistakes, or the suffering that arises from them. Nevertheless, suffering has a definite place in God's overall scheme of things, even though God does not plan specific woes.

Credible though this might sound when we first hear it, we can ask: "Does suffering *really* perfect character?" Where are those people? There are not many saintly Mother Theresa's around! Like the "God is in control" model, how does this view respond to the *massive* amount of suffering in the world? And some of that suffering is due to truly *horrendous* evils, like the Holocaust and other examples of brutal mass genocide, and the sickening massacre in Norway on July 22, 2011. At a more individual level, we hear daily of sexual abuse incidents toward women and children for the twisted pleasure of men; slavery and human trafficking continues. Are the potential benefits that accompany suffering *ever* worth the price? In other words, is this theodicy "cost effective"? It sounds dangerously like it is attempting to justify the unjustifiable. It makes it sound like evil itself isn't so bad after all.[35] It even appears to give evil some dignity, as it assigns a positive role to suffering in God's good creation.[36]

From my own experience—and that of many others—it is fair to say that those who experience suffering *may* also encounter God in profound ways, ones that might not otherwise arise. I have discovered this for myself and so I personally believe Robert Browning Hamilton was right. I have learned through the unwanted path of pain that God's love and the Christian hope is more powerful than evil. Nevertheless, I have a serious problem

see p. 68

---

34. Rice, *Suffering and the Search for Meaning*, 68. The phrase "vale of soul-making" comes from the English poet John Keats (1795–1821).

35. Wright, *Evil and the Justice of God*, 40–41.

36. McGrath, *Christian Theology*, 224; Plantinga et al., *Christian Theology*, 215.

with this "no pain, no gain" theodicy. It seems to me to be an argument from the *few* that is then overgeneralized to the *many*.[37] "What does not kill you makes you stronger" can only be said by winners not losers, "survivors" not "victims." Only the person who, in time, *overcomes* adversity can ever endorse this viewpoint. You never hear it from those who are crushed by suffering. And it can be argued the evidence is overwhelming that this latter group is the vast majority.[38] Furthermore, it is not something to *ever* say to anyone in the midst of suffering or to those who live in chronic pain, or who have a permanent disability. But it is still true to say that someone—like the biblical Joseph—may see for *themselves*, with the help of hindsight, some purpose, or benefit, from their anguish.

In conclusion, there is some wisdom in this "no pain, no gain" outlook, not least its retrospective plausibility for eventual victors. It also resonates with modernism's evolutionary optimism that is embedded within our secular society. Yet it fails to face up to the reality of the horrors of two World Wars. Furthermore, it is a viewpoint that plays into the individualism of Western society. Only *individuals* can claim this to be true in their experience, and it cannot—by induction—be generalized to everyone. Indeed, the evidence of suffering experienced around the world—both its quantity and severity—is a strong and convincing counterargument. I would also add that "no pain, no gain" can all too easy to become a godless rationale for the existence of suffering. It is an analysis that belittles the problem; it does not take the pervasiveness and power of evil seriously enough, nor the immense suffering of the powerless. Consequently, as a stand-alone theodicy it contains dangerous half-truths which, once exposed, make it ultimately unsatisfying.

"An Enemy Has Done This"

Immediately after Matthew presents the well-known parable of the sower (Matt 13:1–9, 18–23), he relates another farming parable of Jesus, namely, the parable of the weeds (Matt 13:24–30, 36–43).[39] The kingdom of

---

37. Hasker, *Triumph of God over Evil*, 218.

38. Consider, from both historical and global perspectives, the extent of the effects of war, economic hardship, famine, disease, disability, abuse—sadly, the list goes on and on.

39. The parable is unique to Matthew, although a highly condensed kernel is found in Mark 4:26–29.

heaven—the reign of God—is likened to a wheat field. But someone sows weeds in the farmer's field during the night and they grow among the good grain. Then

> the slaves of the householder came and said to him, "Master, did you not sow good seed in your field? Where, then, did these weeds come from?" He answered, "An enemy has done this." The slaves said to him, "Then do you want us to go and gather them?" But he replied, "No; for in gathering the weeds you would uproot the wheat along with them. Let both of them grow together until the harvest; and at harvest time I will tell the reapers, 'Collect the weeds first and bind them in bundles to be burned, but gather the wheat into my barn.'"[40]

Matthew writes that Jesus later explains the parable's meaning to his disciples privately: the field is the world, the sower of the good seed is the Son of Man, and the weeds were sowed by the devil (13:37–39). Only "at the end of the age" (13:39-40) will the weeds be separated from the wheat, for fear of damaging the roots of the good seed (13:29). The disciples are nevertheless assured that justice will finally be done at the harvest. That comforting message is also for *now*, since we continue to live in a world that has good and evil in close proximity—indeed, whose very roots are even intertwined, as Solzhenitsyn reminds us at the beginning of the chapter.

A passage like this presents the dualistic worldview during the (late) Second Temple period. There is little reference to Satan in the Old Testament, the most notable mention being in the prologue of Job, where he parades as a divinely appointed "accuser" in the heavenly court.[41] In the bulk of the Old Testament, God is understood to be the source of good and evil.[42] But theological outlooks change and a different view gradually emerges. Satan (or the devil) is mentioned many times in the New Testament—most vividly in the temptations of Jesus in the wilderness.[43] According to the parable of the weeds, evil—opposition to the reign of God—is because "an enemy has done this." C. S. Lewis summarizes this position well:

---

40. Matt 13:27–30.

41. Job 1–2. Other mentions of Satan are: 1 Chr 21:1 and Zech 3:1. Note: I view Job as having a late date since it critiques the widely held views within the earlier wisdom literature tradition—such as Proverbs.

42. See, for example, Isa 30:19–20; 45:5–7; Lam 3:37–38; Job 1:21; 2:10; 42:11.

43. Matt 4:1–11; Luke 4:1–13. See also 1 Pet 5:8; Eph 6:12–13; Rev 12:7–8; 20:2.

> The Christian view [is] that this is a good world that has gone wrong, but still retains the memory of what it ought to have been. . . . One of the things that surprised me when I first read the New Testament seriously was that it talked so much about a Dark Power in the universe—a mighty evil spirit who was held to be the Power behind death and disease, and sin. . . . Christianity thinks this Dark Power was created by God, and was good when he was created, and went wrong. Christianity agrees with Dualism that this universe is at war. But it does not think this is a war between independent powers. It thinks it is a civil war, a rebellion, and that we are living in a part of the universe occupied by the rebel.[44]

Many Christians today believe in the existence of a satanic figurehead; evil then becomes *personalized*. Like for Lewis, I suspect the main reason is "because the Bible tells me so." "Even Jesus speaks of the devil, so such a being *must* exist!" Such a justification is based on the traditional "plain sense" reading of Scripture. That does not mean it is necessarily wrong, but that rationale alone is not one that will convince many today—including other followers of Jesus, like me. (The issue of the reality of the devil is explored briefly in the appendix.) We have already come across such an archenemy of God in the *Christus Victor* atonement metaphor within chapter 3. The seeds for this kind of dualistic thinking, and the resultant cosmic battle, are to be found in the New Testament; this parable is one such text. The origin of human suffering—and the "groaning" of creation (Rom 8:22) discussed in the previous chapter—is, then, simply a feature of this war.

The success of Alvin Plantinga's free will defense led him to propose an extension. What if, in addition to humankind, God also made angelic beings with genuine free will? And what if they were delegated responsibility for running the physical processes in the cosmos? And what if one such angel, a key figure—let's call him Lucifer—led a rebellion against God very early in cosmic history? Then Lucifer and his team could wreak havoc against God's ordered creation and therefore be responsible for all *natural* evil, including disease, decay, and even death itself. All the free will defense's conclusions pertaining to humankind can be extended to Lucifer (Satan) and his demonic followers. Thus *both* moral and natural evil have *free will* as the underlying explanation for the problem of suffering. The free will defense, as it relates to human beings, enjoys respect among

---

44. Lewis, *Mere Christianity*, 42, 45. Lewis first wrote this book in postwar 1952; the rise of the *Star Wars* saga has made such rhetoric less unacceptable, perhaps more plausible even, within postmodern pop culture.

philosophers and theologians. But few are enamored with this extension to angels and demons. For a philosopher, the argument only needs to be logically consistent and *possible*; it need not be *plausible*. But, in a scientific age, no one—including most theologians—seriously wants to invoke angels and demons as the underlying explanation for natural processes. Since Satan and his cohorts are not prominently featured in preexilic Old Testament thought, then to suggest that we *must* believe in this dualistic New Testament worldview as an essential feature of *biblical* Christianity is clearly overreaching.

Nevertheless, it is still essential to take the presence of evil in our world very seriously; this is not a license to belittle it in any way whatsoever.[45] But we must be mindful that Jesus and the New Testament writers were simply using culturally acceptable explanations consistent with their own times—just as the Old Testament authors did many centuries earlier. In that sense the cosmic battle is an *explanation* of reality, not a formal "theory" of reality. Our challenge today is to understand the biblical worldview (as best we can) and faithfully adapt the essence of what the authors inferred in communicating *their* message to *our* contemporary audiences. Their way of thinking was *prescientific* and we cannot expect or impose a simple one-to-one mapping of biblical themes and ideas onto a modern, scientific canvas.

Even so, to say "an enemy as done this" is still a *possible* explanation for the problem of evil. Those who advocate for the "God as warrior" motif often speak of Lucifer as a fallen angel, claiming unequivocal biblical authority for such a view.[46] But, as mentioned above, even the notion of "fallen angels" is only mentioned in passing within Scripture.[47] These incidents are then woven into an elaborate tale creating the basis for an ongoing cosmic war. In this battle, as we have already seen when discussing the traditional *Christus Victor* view of atonement, humankind's role in history is somewhat incidental.[48]

---

45. See Wink, *Powers That Be*; Wright, *Evil and the Justice of God*.

46. See Boyd, *Satan and the Problem of Evil*.

47. See: Luke 10:18, 2 Cor 11:14, 2 Pet 2:4, Rev 12:7–9. Concerning the mention of Satan in Revelation, I advise caution in simply literalizing apocalyptic literature. Moreover, we cannot deny the cultural influence of John Milton's *Paradise Lost*.

48. In one version of the story, Lucifer persistently charges God with being tyrannical and abusive, and hence unworthy of devotion from his creatures. The plan of salvation is God's response to Lucifer, one that is unexpected and meant to reveal God's genuine, loving character. This is achieved by Jesus obediently living a life of suffering service to display God's love and expose the emptiness of the devil's accusations. Is God's "sending

There are, nevertheless, constructive implications in this response to the problem of evil. First, it makes it abundantly clear that suffering does *not* come from God, but from something utterly opposed to God. Moreover, we do not suffer because God *wants* it; God desires the opposite. While I personally think this is obvious, recollect those Christian voices who claimed AIDS was God's judgment on homosexuals, or that natural disasters—like the earthquake in Haiti—were divine retribution on the godless. I suspect some of those Christian leaders would also be comfortable advocating for a cosmic warfare model; if so, you can't then claim that such tragedies are from the hand of God! Why attribute them to God, or blame the victim, if your overarching theological framework is that such things are from the devil? It makes no sense.

Second, there is now no "Why me?" question, for there is nothing *personal* in this view of suffering because God did not plan or micromanage our pain. Instead, creation's suffering is simply "collateral damage" in the cosmic war. Stark as that may sound, this perspective means we need not—even should not—*blame God* for our suffering. As Gregory Boyd puts it, "While we need not assume there is a divine purpose *leading to* our suffering, we can and must trust that there is a divine purpose that *follows from it*."[49] On one level this is helpful and hope-filled, pastoral advice. But note that although this meaning-making conclusion is derived from a very different source, it echoes the same sentiments as John Hick's "vale of soul-making" theodicy, i.e., the overall outcome from suffering is (potentially) beneficial for human growth. In clarification, and in the context of Romans 8:28, Richard Rice adds,

> This doesn't mean that everything is ultimately good. Nothing makes it good that bad things happen. What it means is that God works for good, no matter what happens. God doesn't let suffering have the last word. Instead God responds to every situation in ways that promote growth and healing. God works to bring about something good, no matter how bad things may be.[50]

---

of his son" really to be understood in this light—as saving God's *reputation*? Is this what is meant by divine *love*? And does the devil really have all the powers this view attributes to him? What about continuous creation and God as Sustainer (Acts 17:28; Heb 1:3)? See Rice, *Suffering and the Search for Meaning*, 81.

49. Boyd, *Is God to Blame?*, 196, his emphasis.

50. Rice, *Suffering and the Search for Meaning*, 99.

That said, the key point—in this context—is that the "Why me?" question becomes a nonissue. More generally, one can only propose a response to the "Why me?" question if one can also answer convincingly the "Why *not* me?" question!

Third, God is a God of both *justice* and *love*. God has responded—and is responding—to evil in the world, and we are called to *partner* with God in opposing evil and all its effects. As Matthew 13:37–43 indicates, there is an eschatological dimension to the resolution of the problem of evil. It is fair to say there is some frustration with this "good news" message, because—as painkiller medication adverts continually remind us—we live an age that demands instant relief.[51] Nevertheless it presents a *firm* and *reliable* hope, and—frankly—I find that meaningful hope is nonexistent within secular responses to the problem of suffering. It is a hope that is based on historical events, not just the cross of Christ, but in the repeated pattern of God raising up rescuers in times of need—I will elaborate further in the next chapter. In conclusion, we should embrace all these positive aspects, but we need not place these important affirmations in a dualistic "an enemy has done this" narrative.[52]

"Even God Can't Do Everything"

As we have seen, when suffering happens, people often look for a *purpose* behind it, whether that is because "God is in control" or in order "to perfect human character." Even if those notions of a divine purpose are rejected, many seek comfort in knowing that somehow, somewhere suffering has *meaning*. As Viktor Frankl discovered in the horrors of the Nazi concentration camps, "those who know the *why* for their existence will be able to bear almost any *how*."[53] The "enemy has done this" is one response that provides

---

51. Colin Gunton writes, "As great a mystery as the origin of evil is the time taken to destroy it. In face of this, all we can say is that the nature of its overcoming by the patient obedience of the incarnate Son makes it clear that evil is finally to be destroyed only eschatologically (1 Cor 15). . . . That overcoming is, to be sure, anticipated in the resurrection of Jesus and in our times by the works of the Spirit, who enables particular beings and events to become what they are created to be in the Son. But until then it is only partial and by anticipation." Gunton, *Triune Creator*, 173–74.

52. See also Long, *What Shall We Say?*, 130–51, and Rohr, *Job and the Mystery of Suffering*, 168–71.

53. Adapted from Frankl, *Man's Search for Meaning*, 80.

an overarching context for our suffering. Richard Rice introduces another group's answer:

> Ditch explanations. Don't try to make sense of suffering, just try to get through it. . . . Suffering just happens and that's it. . . . Explanations are neither here nor there. . . . They seem irrelevant to the real challenges of life.[54]

In one sense, surviving the moment is—of course—the only priority in a crisis. Reasons *are* irrelevant. However, later when the drama has subsided and life has become "normalized" again, should we simply give up reflecting on the bigger questions of suffering? Is agnosticism toward suffering truly the "answer"? Must we simply accept that life's unfair, so deal with it and move on—invent meaning if you must?

Rabbi Harold Kushner published the best-selling book *When Bad Things Happen to Good People*. There he rejects any attempts at explanations that try to defend "God's honor, with logical proof that . . . evil is necessary to make this a good world . . . [or] use words and ideas that transform bad into good and pain into privilege."[55] While acknowledging the idea of God weaving a tapestry may be moving and comforting for some, he dismisses it as "wishful thinking."[56] He adds,

> If a human artist or employer made children suffer so that something immensely impressive or valuable could come to pass, we would put him in prison. Why then would we excuse God for causing such undeserved pain, no matter how wonderful the ultimate result may be?[57]

Kushner rejects, like many, the all-powerful, all-controlling God of classical theism and seeks for an alternative where suffering is *outside* of God's will.

His journey of discovery, as most journeys do at some point, leads him to reconsider the book of Job. Kushner outlines the traditional Old Testament worldview and the premises of the key players in the story:

1. God is all-powerful and causes everything that happens.

54. Rice, *Suffering and the Search for Meaning*, 105.

55. Kushner, *When Bad Things Happen*, 4, 23. He also rejects God as causing suffering as a test or as a teachable moment: "If God is testing us, He must know by now that many of us will fail the test. If He is only giving us burdens we can bear, I have seen Him miscalculate far too often" (ibid., 26).

56. Ibid., 18.

57. Ibid., 19.

2. God is just, rewarding the good and punishing the wicked; people get what they deserve.

3. Job is a good person.[58]

Job's friends accepted (1) and (2), and rejected (3). They therefore encouraged Job to acknowledge he wasn't as righteous as he thought he was, and repent. There is obviously an element of "blaming the victim" here.[59] Job, on the other hand, affirmed (1) and (3), and questioned (2). He wanted a fair legal trial to present his case and be vindicated (Job 23:1–7; 31:35). After experiencing his dark night of the soul, God becomes vividly present and—at long last—God's silence is over as he addresses Job in two powerful speeches (Job 38–41). Kushner claims that the *writer* of Job, through the contents of those speeches, affirms (2) and (3):

> Forced to believe in a good God who is not totally powerful, or a powerful God who is not totally good, the author of the book of Job chooses to believe in God's goodness.[60]

He suggests, in the context of God's dealings with the sea serpent Leviathan (Job 41), the ancient symbol of chaos and evil, that "even God has a hard time keeping chaos in check and limiting the damage that evil can do."[61] Even God *can't* do everything.

He goes on to say that because there is randomness in the universe, sometimes shite happens—so to speak—for no reason. Yes, there is order in God's creation, but "pockets of chaos" remain.[62] He adds, using dualistic rhetoric: "Fate, not God, sends us the problem."[63] By stressing the role of randomness, he is claiming that there are *no explanations* for certain tragic events:

> These events do not reflect God's choices. They happen at random, and randomness is another name for chaos, in those corners of the universe where God's creative light has not yet penetrated. And

58. Ibid., 37. See also Rice, *Suffering and the Search for Meaning*, 106–7.

59. Kushner, *When Bad Things Happen*, 39.

60. Ibid., 43.

61. Ibid. Kushner takes God's words to Job in 40:9–14 to mean: "If you think that it is so easy to keep the world straight and true, to keep unfair things from happening to people, *you* try it" (ibid., 43, his emphasis).

62. Ibid., 52. For Kushner, God's brings order out of chaos (*creatio ex materia*), not creates out of nothing (*creatio ex nihilo*)—process theologians agree. See ibid., 51.

63. Ibid., 129.

chaos is evil; not wrong, not malevolent, but evil nonetheless, because by causing tragedies at random, it prevents people believing in God's goodness.[64]

For Harold Kushner, God *is* good—not cruel—but simply limited in what he can do by the laws of nature and our moral freedom. He does not blame God for illnesses, accidents, or natural disasters. He finds that it is easier to worship a God who hates suffering but can't eliminate it, than to worship a God who is in tight control of the universe.[65] While some bad things happen to us for no reason, *we*—not God—can give them meaning and so redeem their senselessness.[66] In the final analysis, Kushner's response to the question, "What good [then] is God?" is simply: "God may not prevent calamity, but He gives us strength and the perseverance to overcome it."[67]

You have to respect books written by those experienced in the dismal trenches of human suffering, even if you don't agree with everything they say. Many people agree with Kushner and one strength of his book is that much of it resonates with the day-to-day practicalities of modern human existence. Yet, like the earlier "what does not kill you makes you stronger" theodicy, there are sufficient half-truths to make it both plausible and dangerous. I agree with many aspects of the book, but find his conclusions shallow and therefore disappointing. I am not the only one.

While I concur with the way Kushner outlines the three options in the book of Job, I don't come to the same conclusion concerning the *writer's* viewpoint. (Given the vast number of books written on Job, that's no great surprise! And there are other ways of setting up those options.[68]) Thomas Long questions whether it is truly an *exegetical* insight of Kushner's and

64. Ibid., 53.

65. Ibid., 134. Richard Rice adds, "Of course the fact that God can't do *everything* doesn't mean he can't do *anything*. . . . The principal way God works in the world is through human beings. When we care for those around us who suffer we show that we are responsive to God's own values and purposes. . . . Because we occupy a different place in the scheme of things *we* can do things God can't." Rice, *Suffering and the Search for Meaning*, 107–8, emphasis mine.

66. Kushner, *When Bad Things Happen*, 136. He also quotes theologian Dorothee Sölle as saying (in her book *Suffering*), "The most important question we can ask about suffering is whom it serves. Does our suffering serve God or the devil, the cause of becoming alive or being morally paralyzed? Not 'where does tragedy come from?' but 'where does it lead?'" (ibid., 137).

67. Kushner, *When Bad Things Happen*, 141.

68. See, for example, Rohr, *Job and the Mystery of Suffering*, 167.

wonders if it is more like *eisegesis*, whereby Kushner reads *into* Scripture what he already believes to be true.[69] Moreover his emphasis on fate and chaos introduces a cosmic dualism which the Judeo-Christian tradition rejects. Fate inadvertently becomes an independent power of causation, rather than no explanation at all.[70] I find Terence Fretheim's nuanced analysis of God's speeches to Job to be more insightful.[71] Since God created the sea monsters, "chaos" is deemed a part of God's *good* creation (Gen 1:21). Randomness and chance are therefore an integral part of the universe, together with what we call the "laws of nature." Both are morally neutral, and both are needed for a *developing* cosmos. Pure order and regularity would be monotonous with endless replication and no novelty; unmitigated randomness is simply total disorder. Of *necessity* we need both; we can't have one without the other. The disorder we see in nature is, then, not defective and/or divinely "mismanaged" creation, rather precisely the kind of world that God intended. Consequently, although the world is good, well-ordered, and reliable, it is also wild, untamed, and not risk-free to humankind—not even for righteous people, such as Job.[72]

It can further be said that, in the two divine speeches, God is challenging Job to recognize the proper nature of creation, and that suffering may be experienced in just such a world quite apart from sin and evil. In so doing, Job may better appreciate what his place and role is within God's world, even in the midst of suffering. Fretheim concludes,

> God will sustain such an ordered and open-ended creation even in the face of the suffering ones who wish that God would have created a world wherein human beings could be free from suffering. That is a price, sometimes a horrendous price, which creatures pay for the sake of having such a world; *but it is also the price that God pays, for God will not remove the divine self from that suffering*

---

69. Long, *What Shall We Say?*, 66.

70. Ibid., 68; Hall, *God and Human Suffering*, 154–55.

71. Fretheim, *God and World*, 233–47. See also Fretheim, *Creation Untamed*; Reddish, *Science and Christianity*, 161–63.

72. Fretheim, *Creation Untamed*, 81–84, 108. He also states, "This creational being and becoming is well-ordered, but the world does not run like a machine, with a tight causal weave; it has elements of randomness and chaos, of strangeness and wildness. Amid the order there is room for chance. . . . Given the communal character of the cosmos—its basic interrelatedness—every creature will be touched by the movement of every other. While this has negative potential, it also has a positive side, for only then is there the genuine possibility for growth, creativity, novelty, surprise, and serendipity." Fretheim, *God and World*, 244.

and will enter deeply into it for the sake of the future of just such a world.[73]

I find this view of God's activity in the world much more potent and hope-filled.

Regardless of the book's many helpful insights, Douglas John Hall finds Kushner's conclusions as "theologically and humanly unsatisfying. He ends . . . with 'religion' being pragmatically useful to sufferers, but it is the sufferer himself or herself who has to derive whatever meaning he or she can from the experience."[74] Consequently, Kushner's approach does not ultimately reflect "the depths of biblical theology" and is a "capitulation to modernity."[75] Thomas Long similarly concludes:

> When one strips away all the biblical language and the pastoral talk from Kushner's book, what remains is fairly stark. We live in a world where random Fate causes suffering and pain, . . . and other than sending out Hallmark-style inspirations for people to have courage and work together, God can do little about it. What is left [is] for good people to . . . face life bravely, with a willingness to accept the hand that reality deals them and to do what they can to make the world better.[76]

He then adds, "Faith promises more." I agree.

Kushner is not the only one to promote the "even God can't do everything" theodicy. Theologian Thomas Jay Oord also advocates for this view, but his reasoning is that God can't do everything because that is the *logical* nature of God's love.[77] What this means is that God *cannot* unilaterally prevent evil, whether caused by human choice or via natural processes, because that is inconsistent with divine love. God cannot interfere, as that would make God controlling and, for Oord, divine love, is—of necessity— "uncontrolling."[78] Moreover, even random events (e.g., mutations, accidents, chance coincidences) *cannot* be prevented by God because they

---

73. Fretheim, *God and World*, 237, emphasis mine.

74. Hall, *God and Human Suffering*, 157.

75. Ibid., 158.

76. Long, *What Shall We Say?*, 69.

77. Oord, *Uncontrolling Love of God*, 94–95, 147, 160–66. Thomas Jay Oord is differentiating between divine self-limitation (*kenosis*), which he regards as *voluntary*, and divine love, which (in his view) logically precedes divine will and power and is the *essential*, primary divine attribute.

78. Ibid., 167–75.

are unplanned and unforeseeable—and a relational God is not "outside" of time but experiences sequences of events in an analogous way to us.

Oord's conclusions are very similar to those of process theology, even if his rationale has a very different starting point.[79] In process theology, God is the source of novelty, change, and order in our incomplete world—one which is still coming into being. God is not just the Instigator or Designer of the order within the cosmos, but influences all that goes on without being the sole cause for any event.[80] Process theology argues *all events* within nature (including human decisions) have the freedom and creativity that God has endowed and God cannot override them; God can only attempt to influence them.[81] Since God is a persuader, he cannot *unilaterally* perform the acts Christians traditionally attribute to God, such as miracles. Instead God works through the laws of nature, human free will, chance, and the freedom he has bestowed within the natural order. Because these entities can only be persuaded and not coerced, then God does not always get his way and so evil can arise for which God cannot be held responsible. In other words, evil is—unfortunately—inevitable, but it is not God's fault! Because God is good, we should be reassured that God is doing his best in the situation.

One analogy, however inadequate, is that of a soccer manager.[82] The manager does not have the capability of physically playing in the match because he simply doesn't have that kind of power. He can influence it from the side lines, but he is not personally responsible for any specific actions of the players. Indeed nothing the players do on the pitch can be attributed directly to the manager's involvement. The manager is genuinely affected by the match, cares deeply about the outcome, and hopes for the best. But the outcome of the match is not in the manager's hands—regardless of how competent and inspirational a manger he is.

Process theists argue that *if* God *is* truly almighty, as those who advocate for "creation-out-of-nothing" claim, then God *should* have been able to make a world without suffering. God evidently didn't—or couldn't. Alternatively, if God is omnipotent—as traditional theists maintain—and

---

79. See also Cobb and Pinnock, *Searching for an Adequate God.*

80. This viewpoint builds on *creatio ex materia,* and regards the cosmos as both necessary and an intimate part of the divine life (i.e., panentheism).

81. Peterson et al., *Reason and Religious Belief,* 163–65.

82. The analogy with a sports manager is adapted from Rice, *Suffering and the Search for Meaning,* 112–13.

has the power to "intervene" and yet doesn't, then that makes God morally culpable for failing to use that power.[83] Either way, God is to blame for everything that goes wrong. The choice we are being presented is between two polarized extremes: "God is in control of everything" (i.e., divine determinism) and "God can't unilaterally do anything"! Both, it seems to me, are too *certain* for the Christian's journey of *faith*. This is a false dichotomy; there has to be nuanced middle ground. Process theism both describes the general action of God *and* denies that God can act in particular ways. I — 引ר maintain that God *is* the God of process, but not *only* the process.

Process theology's "God" also seems too passive in comparison to the biblical portrayal of the Divine. John K. Roth describes it as "God on a leash."[84] It seems to me that this "God" is more like a permeating life-force than the personal Trinitarian God of the Christian tradition. Thomas Long writes,

> There is a ring of truth when the critics complain that process theologians want to draw an empathetic picture of God, but they end up producing merely a pathetic one, a God who might be endearing, but not worthy of worship. Here is God in the midst of chaos, whispering, pleading, trying to persuade . . . but the results are less than impressive.[85]

In our earlier analogy, one wonders if God's influence is not so much like that of a soccer manager as that of a cheerleader in American football! Karl Rahner once said in conversation with Jürgen Moltmann, "To put it crudely, it does not help me to escape from my mess and mix-up and despair if God is in the same predicament."[86] John Polkinghorne's "dissatisfaction" with process theology is that it is insufficiently strong in its portrayal of God's action to make Godself the grounds of reliable [eschatological] hope.[87] The last point concerning hope is very important, particularly in the context of suffering. Will "love win" at the eschaton and all evil be overcome; will

83. Griffin, "Creation, Chaos, and Evil," 117–19. Thomas Jay Oord agrees; Oord, *Uncontrolling Love of God*, 68, 141. See also Rice, *Suffering and the Search for Meaning*, 112–13.

84. Roth, in Davis, *Encountering Evil*, 125. Moreover, John Hick describes process theology's "God" as a "finite God" (ibid., 129).

85. Long, *What Shall We Say?*, 75.

86. Cited in ibid., 76.

87. Polkinghorne, *Faith of a Physicist*, 66–67. He also wonders whether such a God "could be the One who raised Jesus from the dead." See Polkinghorne, "Kenotic Creation and Divine Action," 92.

shalom and wholeness be realized? Persuasion provides no guarantee and, as Long says, the results so far are "less than impressive." This is far too weak an eschatology and Polkinghorne is right to be dissatisfied. If that is indeed the case, then why not eat, drink, and be merry, for tomorrow we die![88]

These critiques of process theism can be applied to all philosophical approaches to the problem of suffering. These can be regarded as arising from a "bottom-up" methodology which, from a foundation that is excessively biased toward resolving the problem, ends up deducing the nature of God. In that regard, it is a modern version of the medieval "god-of-the-philosophers." Nevertheless, I wholeheartedly agree with Douglas John Hall: "Every responsible attempt to rethink the question of 'God and human suffering' . . . must involve in a primary sense a radical reinterpretation of divine omnipotence."[89] We saw this earlier in chapter 2. The issue is *how* we sensitively and wisely formulate that reinterpretation, both in light of the Christ-event and using all four elements of the Wesleyan quadrilateral: Scripture, reason, tradition, and experience. While one cannot lose sight of the healthy—but reactionary—response that rejects the God of classical theism, the outcome of our theological reflections must *not* be, as Long puts it, a "mangling of the doctrine of God."[90] As Hall reminds us,

> God's problem is not that God *is not able* to do certain things. God's problem is that God loves! Love complicates the life of God as it complicates every life. . . . God . . . is not power*less*, [rather, God's] power expresses itself unexpectedly in the weakness of love."[91]

Rage, Protest, and Lament

Television news has brought the plight of the world into our living rooms. A key moment in TV history was the coverage of the sub-Saharan famine in Africa that inspired the original *Band Aid* concert, pioneered by Bob Geldof and Midge Ure. Musicians and the media worked together in an

---

88. See Eccl 8:15; 1 Cor 15:32. This certainly seems to be part of Bart Ehrman's conclusion; Ehrman, *God's Problem*, 277.

89. Hall, *God and Human Suffering*, 155.

90. Long, *What Shall We Say?*, 75.

91. Hall, *God and Human Suffering*, 156, 158, his emphasis.

unprecedented way. Bob Geldof's righteous anger was a powerful force for good. He captured the hearts of the world and shocked international politicians and big business alike with his blunt passion and effectiveness. The sight of starving children on TV moved us all into action, regardless of religious or philosophical worldview. Why? Because everyone knows deep down that the suffering of innocent children *ought not to be*! That was in 1984; we now have twenty-four-hour news channels on cable TV and it is all too easy to become saturated by bad news. We can succumb to compassion fatigue or be overwhelmed by choice as to which good cause to support, but we have no excuse for doing nothing.

Evils like genocide, rape, torture, and other atrocities that plumb the depths of human depravity *should* fill us with rage. Especially when perpetrated against women and children. How else should we respond to the Holocaust and more recent examples of ethnic "cleansing"? It is perhaps worth stating explicitly that the evil humans do to each other and to the environment, both as individuals and corporately, is the *dominant* cause for suffering on our planet. Political scientist Rudolph Rummel estimates that governments have sanctioned more than *250 million murders* over the last century; this is six times more people than died in combat in all the foreign and internal wars during the same time period.[92] Add to those massacres the suffering arising from natural processes, resulting in major catastrophes (e.g., earthquakes, tsunamis, cyclones, famines, floods, etc.) and personal tragedies (disease, genetic abnormalities, cancer—the list is endless), and we wonder: *Why is life so hard for so many?*[93]

Philosophers often distinguish between "moral evil" and "natural evil." The first is the suffering that is as a result of man's choices and actions—and it is often *men*, not women. The second is the pain and anguish due to the impersonal, natural processes discussed in the previous chapter. Insurance companies refer to the latter as "an act of God"! I have come to the conclusion that this abstract distinction is not so helpful. Nevertheless, righteous anger at the existence of suffering is nothing new. The proverbial story of Job is a case in point. But to *whom* is the anger directed? Like Job,

92. See http://www.hawaii.edu/powerkills/20TH.HTM. Rudolph Rummel (1932–2014) introduced the term "democide" for murder by government, which includes genocide, ideological or political motivated killings, and other forms of mass murder. One should reflect on his horrific statistic in the context of Walter Wink's "powers."

93. I can imagine a nomadic family sitting around a campfire in biblical times. A child asks their father that same question, and his reply is the Genesis 3 story!

many express their fury and frustration toward God. They ask, "*Is this the best God can do?*"

Protesting against God in response to suffering, even to the point of cursing him or doubting God's existence, has a long tradition. Not surprisingly, protest (a)theism was spurred on after World War II by Jewish thinkers such as Holocaust survivor Elie Wiesel, winner of the Nobel Peace Prize and author of *Night* (1960). But protest (a)theism was already in the literature in such works as Voltaire's *Candide* (1759), and Fyodor Dostoyevsky's *The Brothers Karamazov* (1880), and Albert Camus's *The Plague* (1947). In one sense these authors were protesting against theism's traditional portrayals of God, whether Christian or Jewish, as one who is all-powerful and perfectly good. Atrocities at the hand of humankind (e.g., cruelty and torture) and nature's destructive curse (e.g., epidemics and the Lisbon earthquake of 1755) rocked their worldviews. God, as understood by a "plain sense" reading of Scripture, was put on trial and found wanting. The sheer waste within history (human and evolutionary) and the existence of vast amounts of horrendous evil was deemed damning evidence against theism's God.

From a Protestant perspective, it was John Calvin's view of God that was on trial—an all-powerful God of perfect goodness who is also all-determining or "in control."[94] Some critics seem to accept God as all-powerful and, consequently, question God's goodness and justice. They hate God's apparent indifference. This was also the biblical Job's complaint. Others' anger leads them to reject God's existence, but they continue to rage at the unfairness of the human experience. For them, and many others, no theodicy can ever be convincing; indeed they are offended by those who even try to justify God in the face of horrendous evil—and rightly so. One should never attempt to make evil sound like it isn't evil, or make it sound like it is part of some secret divine plan that is, in the end, for some "greater good." Suffering is unacceptable—period. And the only appropriate response is to do all one can to alleviate it.

We must respect the sheer honesty of protesting against the existence and persistence of evil. We *should* be outraged. Consider the tragic reality of child abuse. Our protest is because we are claiming passionately that this *ought* not to be so. But there is an irony here. The appeal to "ought

94. It makes little sense for protest (a)theism to be mad at process theism's God. Indeed, process theism can be regarded as one response to protest (a)theism's righteous anger.

not" arguments means humankind as a whole is judging and condemning such actions as morally reprehensible. In so doing, we are appealing to an *objective* moral standard. It is simply *wrong* to abuse children, let alone torture them. The paradox is that the presence of such evil makes us reject or doubt God's existence, but we are appealing to the existence of a *universal* moral law. Ironically, this is an argument for the existence of a good and just God![95]

The Jewish Scriptures contain many references to unjust suffering—not simply in the book of Job. There is a form of literature, known as "lament," that is found readily in the psalms and the prophets.[96] Questioning God's apparent absence and inactivity in times of personal and national trouble came easily to many Jewish writers. Even Jesus himself seemed to require a reason for his sense of abandonment on the cross. Matthew records Jesus as saying, "My God, my God, why have you forsaken me?" (Matt 27:46), which is a quote from a psalm of lament (Ps 22:1). Challenging God in such circumstances was not perceived as sacrilegious or inappropriate, perhaps to the surprise of many Christians today. You can only argue with God if you are in some kind of *relationship* with the Divine, however strained that may be. Raging against God is—perverse as it may seem—a sign of faith! One such man was Habakkuk; his short book begins:

> O LORD, how long shall I cry for help, and you will not listen? Or cry to you "Violence!" and you will not save? Why do you make me see wrongdoing and look at trouble? Destruction and violence are before me; strife and contention arise. So the law becomes slack and justice never prevails. The wicked surround the righteous—therefore judgment comes forth perverted.[97]

And, perhaps shockingly, ends with:

> Though the fig tree does not blossom, and no fruit is on the vines; though the produce of the olive fails, and the fields yield no food; though the flock is cut off from the fold, and there is no herd in the stalls, yet I will rejoice in the LORD; I will exult in the God of my salvation. God, the LORD, is my strength; he makes my feet like the feet of a deer, and makes me tread upon the heights.[98]

95. Rice, *Suffering and the Search for Meaning*, 130–35.

96. For example: Pss 12, 13, 22, 44, 60, 74, 79, 80, 85, and 90, Jer 12:1–4; 15:10, 15–18; 17:14–18; 18:18–23; 20:7–18, and Lamentations.

97. Hab 1:2–4.

98. Hab 3:17–19.

This style is typical of a Jewish lament. Even if the matter is completely unresolved, at the conclusion there is an expression of faith and hope. As one would expect, protest (a)theism doesn't typically end with such a statement of trust in God regardless of the circumstances. The fury remains unresolved. But Jewish writers understood that their covenantal God was big enough to rage against—and gracious enough not to retaliate.

Conclusion: Suffering Never Makes Perfect Sense

There is no one-size-fits-all theodicy; different theodicies give comfort to different people. And the one we hold to now is provisional and likely to change with life experience. As we have seen in these last two chapters, all theodicies have their limits; challenging questions can be asked of each one. We might even want to hold several in tension, based on what we find to be the positive features of each one—or try to develop a hybrid. The result may well not be perfectly coherent; it could even be self-contradictory! Our humanness forces us to recognize that we are not as logical as we think we are; indeed the things we value most, like love and beauty, defy rationality.[99] No rational explanation is perfectly neat and tidy, or completely satisfying. Speaking pragmatically, this means that one's present theodicy is only as good as it is helpful for us at this point in our lives. In the earthquake of suffering, however, the foundations on which we have built our lives get shaken; some may even crumble. Our experience of suffering can be further compounded by a crisis of *faith*. Rather than simply walking away from Christianity, I think it is better to recognize this critical turning point for what it is: a crisis of *theodicy*. In other words, the Christian framework that we are leaning on is not able to support the weight we are placing on it. That underpinning is based on our *present* assumptions concerning the character of God, the nature of creation, and God's action in the world. If our paradigm is failing, we need to discover a God-honoring alternative that better addresses the questions, doubts, and issues we are facing. This is never easy. It is best done in a supportive community; but, sadly, that is frequently not possible because those around us are often also committed to the same theodicy that we now see is not functioning adequately.

---

99. This should not be interpreted as being anti-intellectual or as, in the final analysis, simply dismissing the rational arguments within these last two chapters. Rather, this is an acknowledgment that the human condition is more complex; our behavior is not governed by pure logic. *Star Trek's* Mr. Spock fully appreciated this point!

I liken this scenario to ice floes in the Arctic. The ice is floating over the ocean; it is semistable, not bedrock. When we see fissures rapidly appearing around us, we become acutely aware that our particular ice floe is insecure, drifting, and perhaps even in danger of capsizing. In such situations, we have no choice but to courageously pursue a more stable floe—a different theodicy. In that process, I recommend holding fast to three truths:

1. Suffering is real and suffering is wrong; suffering is never intended by God.

2. The loving, Trinitarian God is not distant, but is present with us as we suffer.

3. Suffering is never the last word.[100]

Although I believe those three statements to be foundational and dependable, in my bones I believe the Christian faith promises *more*. It is to develop that theme that we now turn.

William Hasker points out that, for many, the existence of evil is grounds for *not* believing in God. Theodicies are, from that standpoint, defensive because these philosophical arguments claim that God can *coexist* with evil in the world. But, for the Christian, that is not enough. Christians affirm that "in the end God will *not* coexist with evil but will be gloriously triumphant over it."[101] What might that triumph of God over evil look like? As we have already seen in chapter 3, to respond to that question requires theology, not philosophy. After much thoughtful discussion, Hasker concludes,

> It seems to me that the triumph of good over evil must mean at a minimum that *evil is no longer able to oppose the good*. . . . The broad outlines of the Christian hope are clear, though the details are unknown to us. The world to come is to be a world of fulfilled human lives, free from suffering, death and evil, and permeated with the knowledge and love of God. The evils God's people have

---

100. I acknowledge Rice's excellent pastoral and practical insights in his final chapter: Rice, *Suffering and the Search for Meaning*, 137–64.

101. Hasker, *Triumph of God over Evil*, 200, his emphasis. He adds, "Evil is still very much alive and active; it certainly has not been fully overcome. . . . The nature of evil [is] to *actively oppose* that which is good—it seeks to damage or destroy or corrupt the good" (ibid., 218, his emphasis).

suffered, horrendous evils included, will be . . . engulfed in the experience of intimacy with God.[102]

In order to explore the grounds of that triumph, we must (re)discover the power of *story*. We need to consider the *whole* biblical narrative, not just look to Scripture for specific promises or proof-texts, but to seek a response to the cry of our hearts: "*What is God doing about evil?*"

102. Ibid., 218, 224.

6

What Is God Doing about Evil?

God did not abolish the fact of evil: He transformed it.
He did not stop the crucifixion: He rose from the dead.

—Dorothy L. Sayer

Introduction

The Bible does not tell us about the real origin of evil; it does not
say why the snake was in the garden of Eden—as a *wild* animal,
it should naturally have been outside.[1] Neither does it present a
systematic theology of evil; the references in the Old and New Testaments
need to be appreciated in context of the texts and times themselves and
in the cultural images they utilize. The biblical authors portrayed evil
in different ways (e.g., the sea monster Leviathan, the dragon, the devil,
Satan, and Beelzebub), and they recognized that suffering is often a natural

---

1. The serpent is categorized as a "wild" (rather than domesticated) animal (Gen
1:24–25; 2:20; 3:1, 14) that for some unstated reason is inside the fertile garden. The
origin of this anomaly is unexplained. Incidentally, what the serpent is *not*, at least at this
stage in Old Testament literature, is a euphemism for Satan, the "adversary" or "accuser,"
nor explicitly evil; this connection is made later (e.g., Wis 2:23–24; Rev 12:9; 20:2). See
Conrad, "Satan," 116.

consequence of the decisions we make. But they also made it clear that God abhors evil.

Although the Bible affirms free will, Scripture is nevertheless some-what frustrating to religious philosophers because it does not address their questions in the way they would like. It is also exasperating to Christians and seekers who come to the Bible looking for unambiguous "answers."[2] We have to approach the Bible in a different way. That way needs to be self-critical and self-aware of the assumptions we bring in interpreting the text, and so whatever emerges will have a degree of tentativeness about it. Taking the Bible as a whole, we can look for major themes that flow through the Scriptures and recognize patterns that keep repeating themselves in different guises. In so doing, we may gain insights into suffering as seen through a *theological* lens. Furthermore, if we ask the question, "What is God *doing* about evil?" we can, I think, through the eyes of the various authors, discern a pattern that forms an overarching story line to history and responds to that question. The challenge is to retell faithfully the biblical narrative in a way that can be heard by modern ears.

The Story We Find Ourselves In

The story begins with creation. In Genesis 1 we read the worshipful poem in which God forms the earth by first creating spaces or regions (days 1–3) and then filling those spaces (days 4–6). God brings order out of disorder and nothing resists or prevents the Creator from achieving his purposes. All that God makes is pleasing and delightful to him. It is fit for the in-tended purpose and God declares it "very good." God blesses creation, empowering it to be the "other." He rests on the seventh day and makes it holy. In the second creation account we read of Adam being formed from clay and God breathing the spirit of life into him. God provides for Adam by placing him within a lush orchard. But Adam was alone and God, so the author relates, deemed that inappropriate. So God made all the animals for Adam, and finally created Eve as a suitable companion. We are left with the impression that God regularly visits the couple in the cool evenings to converse with them. So at the very beginning of the narrative we discover God is the Creator and Life-Giver, the one who provides all that is needed

---

2. For example, in Acts 12, Luke makes no comment as to why James was killed and Peter spared.

for life to thrive and who relates personally with humankind. What could be more wonderful! What could possibly go wrong?[3]

In addition to God's provision, we also read of a prohibition; God creates boundaries. Adam and Eve disobey God's instructions and there are consequences—expulsion from the garden of plenty. By their actions they demonstrate that they do not *trust* their Maker and so there is a falling out of relationship between Adam, Eve, and God.[4] That fracture in relationship continues on to the next generation and degrades significantly when Cain kills his brother Abel.[5] Even though some descendants worship God, the general moral decline does not stop. The writer tells us that God deemed the first civilization to be "wicked" and wanted to start all over again with Noah and his family. After the flood, God makes a solemn promise to Noah. Not only would such a catastrophe never happen again (i.e., divine restraint), but God promises seasonal regularity, so providing the necessary stability to cultivate and farm the land.

Within the first few chapters of Genesis, we are already informed that God loves and relates intimately with his creation. God provides, protects, and promises. God knows people's hearts—you cannot hide from God. God also chooses certain people, such as Noah and Abraham, and makes binding promises to them and their families—however flawed they turn out to be as people. God's pledge to Abraham is that his descendants will be a great nation and that all the peoples of the world will be blessed through him.[6] As the narrator tells it, that promise is immediately jeopardized by a life-threatening famine. Moreover, Abraham's wife's (Sarah) inability to have a child was a further challenge to their faith, for how can that promise be fulfilled without a son and heir? In both situations, God rescues them despite their attempts to resolve their plights without reference to divine assistance. Abraham learns to trust in God's faithfulness and in God's ability to fulfill his word in the face of the seemingly impossible. Abraham is an inspirational model of faith and an example for his son's descendants—the nation of Israel. Despite faltering devotion at times, Abraham's trust in God

3. As mentioned in chapter 4, one need not believe in the literal history of early Genesis for its message to be true.

4. In the story, Adam shifts the blame on to Eve (God's provision) and she places the fault on the serpent, i.e., a part of God's creation. Even in the expulsion from the orchard, God provides clothing for Adam and Eve.

5. Even so, God provides a hedge of protection around Cain.

6. Gen 12:2–3.

is remarkable given that the bulk of God's promise could not possibly be realized in Abraham's lifetime.

The twin themes of God's peoples' trust, failure, and repentance on the one hand, and divine provision, promise, protection, and rescue on the other, are repeated over and over again in the Old Testament. The wavering of fallible humankind is contrasted with the loving steadfastness of God. God demonstrates his commitment to keeping his promises to key people in Israel's history, such as Noah, Abraham, Moses, and David. The New Testament builds on this foundation and continues to affirm God's faithfulness and participation in history.

As the people of Israel looked back on their nation's story, they recognized God's provision of key rescuers or saviors. For example, the saga of Joseph tells how, in the end, he saved many from famine—including his whole family. And Moses' liberation of God's people from slavery in Egypt is the nation-defining story of stories. The exploits of military saviors, such as Joshua, Gideon, and Samson, are also relayed as the young nation of Israel strived to take and hold the land of Canaan. Eventually, the nation became like all the others and established a monarchy. With hindsight, nothing equaled the golden age of Kings David and Solomon.[7] As the biblical writers retell Israel's story, not only are the high points of God's provision, protection, and rescue retold, but the narrative is interwoven with the faith journey of the nation and its leaders. The writers were candid. They did not airbrush away the flaws of revered heroes, but detailed their fickleness, foibles, and failures.[8] This mirrors the weaknesses of the people as a whole, which—presumably—was part of the authors' agenda.

Another key point is the establishment of the Ten Commandments following the exodus from Egypt.[9] This formed the basis of the covenant between the emergent nation and their God. It is not that personal relationship with the Divine was to be replaced by—or reduced to—mere rule-keeping; rather peace with God also implies harmony with one's neighbors and with creation. Authentic worship of God, then, has personal, social, and physical consequences. Nevertheless, the practical reality of human nature results in the necessity for rules for collective living. Obedience to the "contract" between Israel and God would result in *blessing.* The consequence

---

7. Even so, there is anti-monarchy sentiment, too—hence high regard for Samuel.

8. The same can be said of the gospel writers' portrayal of the disciples, perhaps especially in Mark.

9. Together with detailed social law, religious regulations and rituals.

of disobedience (e.g., idolatry) would be the opposite: *curse*—the ultimate curse being exile from the homeland.[10]

In addition to judges, priests, and kings, God raised up special individuals—prophets—to act as God's messengers to the monarch and his people. Prophets served as the conscience of the nation, calling the people to repentance and obedience to the one true God, and reminding the leaders of their responsibility to exercise social justice. Even so, we continue to read of the nation's perpetual cycles of diligent obedience and—increasingly and regrettably—of faithlessness and disobedience. Well-meaning fresh starts that, like New Year's resolutions, eventually fade to nothing. Despite the prophets' efforts, the outcome is the breaking up of the nation and, in the end, expulsion from their homeland.

Throughout the history of Israel, the writers portray God as one who relates personally with his people—"the God of Abraham, Isaac, and Jacob." That intimacy, though often strained, is expressed poetically in psalms. Songs of worship and praise are interspersed with psalms of lament that express anguish and their experience of divine silence. At such dark times, the psalmist wonders whether God has forgotten them or, worse, abandoned them. Moreover, throughout Scripture we read of God's fulfillment of his promise through unlikely leaders and in unexpected ways.[11] For example: the youngest son is chosen, rather than the oldest; a king is picked from the least significant tribe; infertile mothers miraculously give birth to sons.[12] Furthermore, God uses people *outside* of the special covenant in very significant ways.[13] There are also inspirational stories of courage and faithfulness in the face of absolute power.[14] Taken altogether, there is clearly an element of unpredictability to God's ways. But the repeated pattern of the

10. See Deut 28 and Lev 26.

11. This aspect is also a feature of modern storytelling. Frodo and Sam are an unlikely duo to perform their saving task in *The Lord of the Rings*. Lucy, the youngest sibling, is most sensitive to the heart of Aslan in the *Chronicles of Narnia*. Harry Potter is a surprising savior in the J. K. Rowling's best-selling saga of good and evil.

12. Sarah, Hannah, and Elizabeth give birth to Isaac, Samuel, and John the Baptist, respectively. Furthermore, Jesus' disciples are a most unlikely bunch to spread the gospel, and Paul's past makes him a dubious choice for ministry (cf. Moses). Moses, Gideon, and many of the prophets lacked self-confidence and apparently needed an empowering "call narrative" to persuade them into leadership.

13. Such as Ruth, Rahab, and King Cyrus; add to that list the Egyptian princess who saved baby Moses and, later, Moses' father-in-law, Jethro, who provided wise advice.

14. For example, David and Goliath, Daniel, Esther, Nehemiah, and the trio Shadrach, Meshach, and Abednego.

people's faithlessness and disobedience is depressingly predictable—and the Babylonian exile is understood in the context of covenant.[15]

But even in that tragedy, God provides prophets and, eventually, a savior. In contrast to the confrontation between Moses and Pharaoh, Nehemiah receives permission from the Persian King Cyrus to take a contingent from the now conquered Babylon back to the Jewish homeland. Nevertheless, even when Jerusalem's walls and temple are rebuilt, the past glory days do not automatically return.[16] The Old Testament therefore ends with disappointment. Before long the Greek and, later, Roman Empires would overrun the land and oppress the people—*again*. The flame of hope has all but gone out as the people wait for yet another deliverer.

The New Testament begins with good news. Not only has a new prophet arisen in John the Baptist, but his message announced the coming of the long-awaited Messiah. With the demise of the two kingdoms, compounded further by the exile, prophetic voices spoke of yet another savior. It was naturally assumed that this special savior—the Messiah—would finally restore Israel to its former glory, thereby being a worthy successor to King David. The gospel writers were convinced Jesus was (and is) that Messiah. He came at a time when the spirit of the law had been forgotten and the rules had become fossilized within legalism, creating burden instead of freedom. Jesus radically reinterpreted the law in the Sermon on the Mount, echoing Moses on Mount Sinai.[17] Jesus announced good news of forgiveness, liberation, and that God's reign was at hand—ironic, given the Roman occupation. His miracles gave a glimpse of the reality of *shalom*: peace with God, one's neighbor, and creation. Those mighty deeds acted as signs, a foretaste of much more to come. God's reign had definitely begun, but *this* kind of kingdom was not what the people expected. In the end, such good news was threatening to those in power, both religious and secular. Jesus, deemed a blasphemer and agitator by the Jewish establishment, was unjustly crucified by the Romans for sedition.

There the story could have ended; but it didn't. God continues to act in surprising ways. Jesus is witnessed to be truly alive again and meets with many of his followers for a time. Fleming Rutledge is unequivocal: "*If Jesus*

15. Consequently, the Old Testament authors saw their sufferings as coming from the hand of God, analogous to parental discipline of willful, wayward children.

16. The earlier prophet Ezekiel had a powerful vision of the spirit of God departing from the temple (Ezek 10–11). But even though the temple is now rebuilt, God's glory had not returned.

17. A literary theme within Matthew's Gospel is Jesus as a new Moses figure.

had not been raised from the dead, we would never have heard of him."[18] The bodily resurrection of Jesus is, then, the pivotal hinge of the story—and of history.[19] Just as the spirit of the prophet Elijah was deemed to be upon his successor Elisha, so the Spirit of Jesus was upon his followers—men, women, young, and old. The apostles spoke with persuasion and boldness, and further miracles were performed so demonstrating the continuing reign of God. Moreover, that good news message of forgiveness and whole- ness was now extended to the entire world, so fulfilling God's promise to Abraham—that *all* the peoples of the world would be blessed through him.

How will the story end? We have journeyed from creation through the Fall (humankind's failure to trust God), to promise and rescue, and are moving toward history's final completion. This "completion" is not "resto- ration," a going *back* to the beginning again, although there are elements of renewal in the eschaton.[20] Rather, just as the God's promises—covenants— were both continuous and discontinuous with previous ones, so the "new heaven and new earth" will be connected with our present reality—but also different. We don't really know or understand what that completion will look like. But we journey onward in faith, trusting in the faithfulness of a capable and good God, one who has continually been recognized as being involved in history and within creation. *This is the meaning-making story we find ourselves in.*[21]

Although there are repetitive cycles in the story, the underlying plot- line is both linear and purposeful—from the beginning toward the comple- tion of the divine goal. If we are honest with ourselves, we should recognize our own faithlessness toward God, and so identify with that aspect of the

---

18. Rutledge, *Crucifixion*, 31, her emphasis. She later states: "It is in the crucifixion that the nature of God is truly revealed. Since the resurrection is God's mighty transhis- torical Yes to the historically crucified Son, we can assert that the crucifixion is the most important event that ever happened." Ibid., 44, her emphasis.

19. While the resurrection is pivotal, so is the *whole* life of Jesus: his birth, teaching, deeds, death, resurrection, and ascension—the Christ-event.

20. It is fair to say that the eschatological hope is sometimes portrayed as a *return* to the garden of Eden in Scripture in the sense that harmony with God and nature will be restored. However, if that were literally the case, then all our suffering would be in vain.

21. There are other important layers and themes one can weave into this narrative, such as tabernacle/temple, Passover, sacrifice, priesthood, prophecy, and kingship, all of which add further richness to the tapestry. Significant elements though they undoubt- edly were in first-century Palestine, such as Jesus' death being viewed as final sacrifice, the lack of such ritual in our modern society means that we struggle to identify with that aspect of the narrative today. See also Wright, *Simply Jesus* and *Revolution*.

story. If we choose to place ourselves within that narrative and consider it a true description of history—as I do—then we can joyfully receive its message of forgiveness and hope.[22] We are then called to partner with God, in the power of the Spirit, to bring about *shalom*, i.e., to participate in the divine purpose of history and undo the consequences of the Fall.

From the beginning, God wanted to be an intimate part of our lives— as illustrated in the Adam and Eve story. We have the choice to trust God or reject him and his ways. History shows us that despite the spectacular achievements of the human intellect, the inherent weakness of being human means we cannot cope with our God-given freedom. If we are wise, we will recognize that we can't make sense of life without recourse to our Maker. True happiness, then, comes from being in relationship with God, not as independent masters of our own destiny.

What Is God Doing about Evil?

Having painted a canvas with a very broad brush portraying the biblical narrative, we can reflect further on what precisely God is doing about evil. As a starting point, I find the story of Noah insightful in this regard. The narrator describes God's viewpoint in disturbingly chilly tones:

> The LORD saw that the wickedness of humankind was great in the earth, and that every inclination of the thoughts of their hearts was only evil continually. And the LORD was sorry that he had made humankind on the earth, and it grieved him to his heart.[23]

This follows from an understanding that God is holy and, consequently, detests evil. The flood story was understood as God's judgment on evil. God's righteous passion was so aroused that he literally went to *war* against the world he had made. Divine anger resulted in God moving to "uncreate"

22. William Hasker comments, "It is not to be expected that secular critics will find the Christian story easy to believe; faith, after all, is a gift from God. But those who find themselves unable at this juncture to believe the story may at least get a better understanding of what is at stake in either believing or rejecting it." Hasker, *Triumph of God over Evil*, 200. I would add that there is also a sense that faith is a *choice* as to whom or what to trust. We can choose to believe in a worldview that is centered on the Trinity, rather than ourselves or some other philosophy. After recognizing God's grace toward us and having become immersed within a Trinitarian perspective, we discover that all good things come from God—including faith and love. While ultimately faith is a "gift from God" (Eph 2:8), it nevertheless requires nurturing.

23. Gen 6:5–6.

the world. He unleashed the waters he had previously restrained in creating the dry land (Gen 1:6–10). He wanted to start all over again, this time beginning with Noah and his family. Although—so the story tells us—the world was destroyed by the flood, God's reaction is telling:

> The LORD said in his heart, "I will never again curse the ground because of humankind, *for the inclination of the human heart is evil from youth*; nor will I ever again destroy every living creature as I have done. As long as the earth endures, seedtime and harvest, cold and heat, summer and winter, day and night, shall not cease."[24]

Despite God's realization that evil will continue to be present within the human heart, even in Noah's family, he promised to exercise divine restraint. As a sign that the divine "war" with humankind was permanently over, he hung up his weapons in the sky never to be used again (Gen 9:13; the rainbow is literally a "bow"). Echoes of God's original blessing of Genesis 1 are to be heard in God's promise to Noah and his descendants.[25]

God still hates evil, but he radically changes his approach in dealing with it.[26] God becomes more "hands-on." God rolls up his sleeves, so to speak, and engages a messy world in order to fix it. God desires to bless the world with his provision, presence, promise, and pardon. This blessing is mediated through Abraham, Israel, and—ultimately—Jesus, and given to the entire world. Surprising as it may seem to us, God also *restrains* evil so that it cannot do its worst.[27] Furthermore—as the biblical authors bear witness—God also *rescues*, the exodus being the prime Old Testament example. God *releases* his people from captivity, not just from slavery in Egypt or from the exile, but from bondage to the power of evil which dominates our lives. This message resonates with—and is reiterated by—many Christians today who testify to the Spirit's continuing transformation of their lives into a "new creation."[28]

As a brief digression, though important to us moderns who view the physical world through the eyes of science, it is necessary to make a

---

24. Gen 8:21–22, emphasis mine.

25. Gen 9:1–17.

26. In the previous chapter, we learned more of divine patience in this matter when discussing the parable of the weeds. Consider too the waiting, longing father in the parable of the lost son (Luke 15:11–32).

27. Wright, *Evil and the Justice of God*, 55.

28. 2 Cor 5:17.

connection between "moral" and "natural" evil. The Old Testament world was holistic; humankind is part of creation—not *above* it—and *shalom* entails a right relationship between God and *all* creation. In this worldview, there are consequences for moral evil (the decisions we make and actions we take that are contrary to God's desires) that impact upon the natural order. As N. T. Wright puts it,

> The evil that humans do is integrated with the enslavement of creation. This is seldom a matter of one-on-one cause and effect, but there is a nexus, a web of rippling events that spreads out from human rebellion against the Creator to the out-of-joint-ness of creation itself. In the same way, when humans are put back to rights, the world will be put back to rights.[29]

Isaiah's eschatological vision of the wolf and the lamb together, and being led by a child (Isa 11:6–9) needs to be understood in that context.[30] From a scientific viewpoint, such holism seems bizarre and incredulous. But rather than getting sidetracked by *literal* interpretations, see this in the context of the overall narrative. The authors understood God to be working to undo *all* the permeating effects of evil. This not only means bringing harmony and tranquility to the natural order, but giving humans a *new* heart for God.[31] At the eschaton, then, God will be all in all (1 Cor 15:28), and heaven and earth will be one with God dwelling among his people (Rev 21:1–4). This is a radical *recreation* indeed, one that refashions—not scraps—this creation that God declared "very good." From a scientific point of view it is hard to imagine how that vision of the eschaton will come about. Some may therefore want to scoff at the biblical metanarrative as naive and outdated. I suggest that—in addition to having faith in a *Creator* who is bigger than our finite minds—we look for further signs of divine action in addressing evil within Scripture. This brings us back to Jesus, the Messiah.

---

29. Ibid., 72.

30. See also Isa 65:17–25. Not only will carnivores become vegetarians again (a reference to the garden of Eden), but even children can play with snakes without fear. All this arises because *shalom* implies an undoing of the effects of the original "curse." Note too that this vision immediately follows the messianic prophecy of Isa 11:1–5. It should also be noted that those Christians advocating for an escapist eschatology, whereby heaven is a place of disembodied spirits (and so abandon the physicality of this world), have been more influenced by a platonic worldview than by the Bible.

31. See Ps 51:10; Jer 24:7; Ezek 11:19; 36:26–27; John 3:3–9; 2 Cor 5:17. The notion of a "new heart" needs to be seen in the light of Gen 6:5, quoted earlier.

In chapters 2 and 3 we considered the Christian doctrine of the Trinity. From this perspective, the incarnation is another surprising act of God, one that reveals the extent of God's love and commitment to the world. But how does the coming of Jesus relate to the original question: "What is God doing about evil?" First, let's consider Jesus' actions and behavior, which are simply him living out his message. Then—in light of that—we will again look briefly at his crucifixion and resurrection.

The miracles of Jesus should not been seen as publicity stunts to provide a platform for preaching, or "proof" of his identity. Rather those mighty deeds were a *sign* of the veracity of his message—that the kingdom of God is here; it's begun. Moreover, Jesus told people, "Your sins are forgiven," a statement that astounded the onlookers as only God could forgive sins. But if you are now at peace with God, then the effects of being liberated from evil should be *holistic*. It should come as no surprise, then, that physical healings are a reversal of the body's "out-of-joint-ness" (see Mark 2:1–12). Furthermore, Jesus had a habit of touching the untouchables— those deemed ritually "unclean"—and thereby risking defilement by physical contact. Yet when Jesus touched the person with leprosy or the woman with the hemorrhaging condition, they were healed; when he touched a corpse, the dead person came back to life (Matt 8:1–4; Luke 7:11–17; 8:40– 56). Instead of Jesus being contaminated or made impure, his wholeness and vitality was transferred to them. In light of this observation, reconsider the line in Isaiah 53:4—referring to the suffering servant—"surely he has borne our infirmities and carried our diseases." It is as if through touch, their disability, disease, and death, was transferred to Jesus . . . and he carried that burden to the cross.

In the Old Testament, the very presence of God was associated with the ark of the covenant, situated first in the tabernacle and, later, in the temple. This holy place is to be contrasted to the locations frequented by Jesus. To the annoyance of the Jewish religious establishment, Jesus ate with loathed tax collectors (Mark 2:14–15; Luke 5:27–29; 19:1–10), and had his feet washed and perfumed by a woman with a dubious reputation (Luke 7:36–50). He also initiated a conversation with a lone Samaritan woman at a well (John 4:1–42), violating cultural taboos and associating with a race the Jews despised. For all this—and more—Jesus was labelled "the friend of sinners" (Matt 11:19). This conduct did not fit in with the Jewish expectations of a holy prophet; even John the Baptist's bizarre habits were more tolerable! Through a Trinitarian lens we see this behavior is a radical change in God's *modus operandi*. The incarnate Son of God chose to hang out with the "wrong" kind of people—the outsiders and marginalized. Yet he was not made impure by this association. Instead, Jesus brought the presence of the Divine to those most in need of being made whole, and brought them back into community (Mark 2:16–17; Luke 5:30–32). Jesus took upon himself their shame and the causes of their exclusion . . . and he carried them to the cross.

Most sermons I hear on the topic of the cross are about *personal* forgiveness. My "sin," or my "missing the mark," was placed upon Jesus at the cross. This transferal is analogous to the innocent, unblemished lamb used in the Jewish sacrificial system as a substitute for *my* own sin, one that provides the means for *my* cleansing.[32] As we saw in chapter 3, another first-century image of the cross was that of a slave being liberated by someone else who was prepared to pay the ransom price to the owner. This metaphor is also often regarded in an individualistic way; Jesus' death somehow releases the person from their bondage to sin.[33]

Biblical though these images undoubtedly are, the death and resurrection of Jesus are *more* than this. They are the ultimate answer to the question "What is God doing about evil?" Those metaphors make sense in a *Jewish* framework because—for Christians—Jesus was the *suffering Messiah* (see Isaiah 53). But the complete connection between the Messiah and the second person of the Godhead did not come about until later. After all, the gospel writers would have had a hard time persuading Jews of the divinity of Jesus since, for them, that would assuredly be blasphemy. But the reality of the resurrection challenged the New Testament writers to rethink all they held dear in their religious outlook and, in so doing, provided the seeds for others to develop a "high" Christology—as discussed in chapter 2. As contemporary Christians, we see the Scriptures through a *Trinitarian* lens and, therefore, in the incarnation, Jesus gathers all that is evil and wrong in the world (sin, shame, brokenness, bondage, disease, disability, and even death itself) and takes it upon himself—as he literally carries his cross to Golgotha. God rescues once more—this time in person—and allows the worst the world can do to fall upon the *whole* Godhead. God has always taken responsibility for the kind of world God created, but in the cross the Trinity demonstrated the extent of the divine willingness to bear that responsibility. In Jesus' ministry, the Son faithfully revealed the divine

---

32. See John 1:29; Rom 3:23–25; Eph 5:2; Heb 9; 1 John 2:2; 4:10; 1 Pet 2:21–24.

33. See Mark 10:45; 1 Cor 6:20; 7:23; Rev 5:9.

heart to humankind; we responded by publicly shaming and killing him. In the way Jesus approached his trial and death, he practiced what he had preached.[34] On the cross, as N. T. Wright puts it, "Jesus suffers the full consequences of evil: evil from the political, social, cultural, personal, moral, religious and spiritual angles all rolled into one; evil in the downward spiral hurtling towards the pit of destruction and despair."[35] Moreover, God the Father witnessed the suffering of the beloved Son and experienced the profound anguish of a devoted parent. The loving, life-giving Spirit shared in the Father's sorrow and the Son's agony, and experienced the Son breathing his last and yielding to death. The united Trinity experienced the full extent of evil—even *death* itself, the anti-creation.[36] Seen in this way, the cross is *bigger* than the sum of all humankind's wrongdoing, enormous though that is. In our holistic picture, the cross also embraces all that is now evil *in creation* including all the natural distortions that oppose life in all its fullness.[37]

The resurrection is the Divine's "*No*" to evil; God *deals* with it, personally. In the resurrection God promises—and *demonstrates*—that evil will *not* have the last word. A potent, bodily resurrection is necessary to counter both the real, physical consequences and the pervasive extent of evil.[38] Something radically novel was witnessed by Christ's followers, and world history has never been the same since. We need not get too distracted by the details of the resurrection body. Taking the texts at face value, Jesus'

---

34. Among other things, nonviolence was a feature of his message. N. T. Wright points out, "When Jesus suffered, he did not curse, and when he was reviled, he did not revile in return (1 Pet 2:23). 'Father, forgive them' (Luke 23:34): that constitutes a radical innovation in the long and noble tradition of Jewish martyr stories, where (as, for instance, in 2 Maccabees 7) the heroes, while being tortured to death, call down God's vengeance on their persecutors and warn them of coming judgement." Wright, *Evil and the Justice of God*, 88–89.

35. Ibid., 92.

36. In addition to experiencing physical pain, as Jesus was tortured before being crucified, there were the human elements of betrayal, abandonment, rejection, manipulation, lies, denial, and hatred. The added irony of John 19:15, where the chief priests (mediators between the Jewish people and God) proclaim to Pilate: "We have no king but the emperor" is simply staggering. It is nothing short of a rejection of the covenant. (Hear too the echo of 1 Sam 8:4–30.)

37. See John 10:10; Col 2:6–10. Note too that the gospel writers' report the temple curtain as being torn in two on Good Friday, not Easter Sunday (Mark 15:38; Matt 27:51).

38. Within the overall biblical story line, this is quite plausible. A "spiritual" or nonphysical resurrection does not answer the effects of sin within the natural order. Ironically, perhaps, this "liberal" view is paralleled by "conservatives" advocating an escapist (even nonphysical) eschatology.

post-resurrection body was both continuous and discontinuous with the physicality of his pre-resurrection body.[39] God's triumph over death also signifies a victory over all the systemic powers (political, military, social, cultural, religious, and even demonic) that placed Jesus on the cross. Nevertheless, we observe that God's ultimate defeat of evil was achieved *through* suffering love; as Thomas Long says,

> Here is the paradox: The love of God, seemingly so weak on the cross, ends up victorious and ultimately destroys the power of evil. . . . The nonviolence of God's love ultimately does violence to evil.[40]

Conclusion

Much more can be—and has been—said on this matter. The key points I am stressing here are: (a) to embrace the Christ-event in a *Trinitarian* way and (b) to recognize our place within a much bigger narrative. A Trinitarian view shows just how much God cares for creation. It counters the legacy of deism that continues to influence our age; God is *not* distant or disinterested, but intimately involved in history—in our suffering world. It also emphasizes that the Father, Son, and Spirit are continually working *together*. Second, the persuasive power of storytelling provides context and perspective. I believe a true, meaning-making (hi)story is more inspiring than a philosophy.[41] While submitting to the truth of the biblical metanarrative is a step of faith, it is not a leap into the dark.

In the end, we all know that suffering is *the* universal experience, and that the biblical narrative is not a simplistic panacea. Despite the cross and resurrection, we still experience pain and suffering in the "now-and-not-yet" kingdom of God. And we wonder why we do not experience more miracles. These are complex issues that need to be explored and given a response—albeit a preliminary one. Nevertheless, if we are convinced of the reality of the overall narrative, *that God has definitively addressed the*

---

39. For further discussion, see Wright, *Surprised by Hope*, 43–44; 148–63.

40. Long, *What Shall We Say?*, 145.

41. Incidentally, C. S. Lewis found the notion that the Christ-event was a "true myth" profoundly instrumental in his own faith journey. For Lewis, the critical difference was that the Christ-event was *not* just like any cultural story or folklore, but was *a myth that really happened* and through which God communicated to humankind; see Downing, *Most Reluctant Convert*, 147–48, 156.

problem of evil—and continually works to vanquish its effects, then we can then live in faith, hope, and love as we carry our own sufferings, and their scars, and journey on toward the eschaton.

Matt 17:20
if u "- had faith (the size of mustard seed) => action
    - need prayer + fasting .

7

Glimpses of the Future in the Present

Miracles are not contrary to nature, but only contrary
to what we know about nature.

—St. Augustine

The most wonderful thing about miracles is that they happen.

—G. K. Chesterton

Introduction

In the previous chapter, mention was made of the miracles of Jesus (and the early church) as being a sign of the presence of the God's reign, or, using a Jewish term, of *shalom*.[1] They pointed to God being powerfully at work and were a manifestation of the long-awaited time of liberation that is a feature of the kingdom of God.[2] We are left with the obvious question: If God is still reigning—as Christians affirm—why don't we witness more miracles today? Or more personally, why wasn't my wife, Anne, healed?

1. See Wright, *Jesus and the Victory of God*, 190–93.
2. See Luke 4:18–19; 7:18–23.

There are various ways to approach these questions. I have reviewed the broader concerns that some have on scientific and philosophical grounds elsewhere.[3] I won't go through those arguments here, but a brief summary is appropriate by way of introduction.

The word "miracle" is typically understood within the context of the lingering Newtonian legacy of a clockwork universe. Within that deterministic worldview, the cosmos is a *closed* system governed rigidly by the laws of nature. From a Christian perspective, those "laws" are divinely instigated, or—more poetically—"the customs of God." That being the case, a transcendent God can only act within such a system by divine *intervention*. In other words, by breaking some of his own laws and *interfering* with the otherwise smooth running of the cosmos. Within this context, then, a miracle is seen as a "supernatural" intrusion into the natural order.

However, the well-established findings of modern physics have undermined conclusively that deterministic worldview. Moreover, scientific "laws" are now known not to be as unbreakable or universal as originally (or commonly) perceived. They *describe* what has happened and do not unambiguously *prescribe* what *must* or *will* happen in all circumstances. Instead of the certainty that was associated with the previous mechanistic worldview, there is recognition of a real element of indeterminacy and openness that is an inherent feature of creation. In light of that, John Polkinghorne points out,

> The problem of miracles is not strictly a scientific problem, since science speaks only about what is usually the case and it possesses no *a priori* power to rule out the possibility of unprecedented events in unprecedented circumstances.[4]

A miracle, by definition, is unprecedented, unrepeatable, and not what one would normally expect. I also agree with the conclusions of Evans and Manis:

---

3. See Reddish, *Science and Christianity*, 125–38, for further details, including a discussion on what we mean by "miracles."

4. Polkinghorne, *Quantum Physics and Theology*, 35. Elsewhere he adds, "Too glib an evocation of special providence may trivialize God's action in the world, but the rejection of all such particular action reduces God to an impotent spectator. The religious mind strives to maintain some balance. . . . The paradoxes of providence are not mere intellectual puzzles. They arise from the heart of religious experience." Polkinghorne, *Science and Providence*, 51.

There is no compelling reason to use the phrase "laws of nature" only to describe laws that hold without exception. . . . It seems rash, therefore, for philosophers or others to claim dogmatically that miracles *cannot* happen. Miracles seem *possible* at least, and it also seems possible for there to be compelling evidence for their occurrence—evidence of the ordinary historical kind.[5]

For a variety of reasons determinism is dead, both philosophically and scientifically. Nevertheless, its influence lingers on in our consciousness, as illustrated in the wide usage of words like "intervention" and "supernatural." We need to be mindful of such sensibilities as they can also influence our theology. The word "miracle" still has popular connotations of God breaking *into* our world from the outside. The biblical words used, however, do not carry that meaning. As N. T. Wright puts it,

They indicate, rather, that something has happened, *within* what we could call the "natural" world, which is not what would have been anticipated, and which seems to provide evidence for the active presence of an authority, a power, at work, not invading the created order as an alien force, but rather enabling it to be more truly itself.[6]

Miracles should *not*, then, be regarded as divine *intervention*, since God is continuously and intimately involved in his creation! Nevertheless, such events are most unusual.

Toward a Theology of Miracles

Moving miracles from the category of "impossible" to "possible" is, in the minds of most Christians, a step in the right direction! Nevertheless, how do we move forward and formulate a positive theology of miracles for today? It is not easy. This is not simply because authentic miracles are inherently rare, but because theologians desire divine action to be coherent. After all, the *same* God who enables the miraculous is also responsible for the entire

---

5. Evans and Manis, *Philosophy of Religion*, 135, emphasis mine. Peterson et al. come to essentially the same conclusion: "It is true that the miraculous is a complex concept, and it is true that serious theoretical and practical questions concerning our ability to identify 'miracles' do exist. But nothing . . . indicates that theists cannot in principle justifiably believe that miracles can occur, or even that miracles have actually occurred." Peterson et al., *Reason and Religious Belief*, 209.

6. Wright, *Jesus and the Victory of God*, 188, his emphasis.

cosmos and its complex, interrelated processes.[7] We must wrestle honestly and responsibly with this issue because of its theological *and* pastoral importance. For those who are suffering, the stakes can be especially high, as a miracle is often deemed to be the last hope. Consequently, some caution is needed. Fascination with "signs and wonders" is nothing new,[8] but we demean our relationship with the triune God if we become miracle-chasers.

In exploring this topic, I have found the views of philosopher-theologian Keith Ward to be helpful. He points out,

> It is quite unsatisfactory to think of miracles as just rare, highly improbable physically inexplicable events. The theist has no interest in the claim that anomalous physical events occur. The events in which the theist is interested are acts of God; and Divine acts do not occur arbitrarily. . . . They have a rationale; and that rationale must be connected with the purposes of God for the world.[9]

Ward highlights that it is not the occurrence of the miracle itself that is so critical, but its *theological significance* in the context of the overall "purposes of God for the world," which were outlined in the previous chapter. Too often we are focused, for one reason or another, on devising a physical explanation for a miraculous event and we overlook the divine message or rationale behind such an incident. This is what is meant by a "theology of miracles."

Miracles (the Greek words used in the New Testament mean either "mighty deeds" or "signs") are a work of the Spirit (Rom 15:18–19), who is likened to the wind.[10] An obvious feature of the wind is its unpredictability. One of the shocking aspects of the coming of the Spirit at Pentecost was the *kind* of people who were anointed. From a Jewish perspective, God's special presence was identified with key leaders, such as royalty (e.g., Samuel's anointing of Saul and David) and prophets, not the common person. In Acts 2 we read of the lavishness of God; the Spirit filled *all* present at the time, regardless of age, gender, or social status. In Peter's first sermon, he

---

7. In more formal language, coherence is sought for in divine action within both "general" and "special" providence.

8. 1 Cor 1:22–24; Matt 12:39; 16:4.

9. Ward, *Divine Action*, 176.

10. See John 3:8; Acts 2:2. Miracles are, of course, a work of the *Trinitarian* God; nevertheless, too often the Spirit's ongoing presence and activity is overlooked. See also Brown, *Miracles and the Critical Mind*, 325.

explained this oddity as a fulfillment of a prophecy of Joel.[11] Later in Acts 10:1–11:18, we read of Peter's astonishing encounter with Cornelius. Cornelius was a *non*-Jew who was dramatically filled with the Spirit, thereby forcing the early church to rethink its theology. These examples suggest that those who have well-defined expectations as to *how* God works should be cautious—the Spirit may surprise us! The occurrence of miracles comes under this umbrella; hence whatever I say must be regarded as provisional.

As mentioned earlier, the physical universe is not a closed, clockwork system, but has a degree of openness within its unfolding processes. From a theological perspective, God has enabled creation to be the "other" and given it room to become so, but its autonomy is relative to the Creator—who is the ultimate source, sustainer, and goal of all things. Keith Ward again:

> If nature is an open, emergent and transcendently oriented set of physical systems, there is little reason to exclude the activity of God as a positive causal factor in the ways things go. . . . On rare occasions . . . material objects may transcend their natural powers as to become awe-inspiring sacraments and vehicles of the Divine. They will thus be, not mere anomalies in an autonomous nature, *but epiphanies of the Spirit, showing the underlying nature and the final destiny and purpose of the material order.*[12]

In this view not only do "epiphanies of the Spirit" reveal the Trinity at work, but we see that miracles can be understood as *glimpses of the future in the present.* I find this view of the miraculous insightful; consider Jesus' resurrection, for example, in this light. This provides a broad *theological* rationale for the miraculous and brings to the forefront of the mind exactly what a Christian's prayer request implies. Furthermore, it also provides an explanation for the scarcity of miracles even in this (post-Pentecost) age of the Holy Spirit. Miracles, then, are not about "proof," but are profound *signs of grace* that vividly illuminate God's purposes in the world. They arise in individuals and communities who have a dynamic relationship with a personal God, who continues to be passionately engaged in the world he made. Miracles are, therefore, only recognized as such with the eyes of

---

11. See Joel 2:28–29; Acts 2:17–18.

12. Ward, *Divine Action*, 178, emphasis mine. John Polkinghorne writes, "Miracles [are] perceptions of a deeper rationality than that which we encounter in every day, occasions which make visible a more profound level of divine activity. They are transparent moments in which the kingdom [of God] is found to be manifestly present (Matt 11:2–6)." Polkinghorne, *Science and Providence*, 60.

faith.[13] In light of this bigger picture, then, miracles are not only possible but probable.[14]

While some Christians might find this preliminary theology of miracles as too cautious, I believe it provides a rational complement to faith—one that is faith *enhancing* and provides *confidence* to pray. Consequently, one can reexamine the miracles of Scripture with openness as to their actual occurrence, but with a critical scrutiny as to each one's theological significance. In particular, since miracles were an important feature of Jesus' reputation, it makes no sense to dismiss them *en masse* as mythical.[15] While we know miracles will be rare, by definition, we have grounds to expect clusters of them to occur where the Spirit of God is discerned to be particularly active. The New Testament evidence suggests this is more likely to happen at the "cutting edge" of kingdom of God activities where systemic evils are being confronted. I see no biblical, theological, or scientific reason why that should not still be the case today. Anthony Thiselton summarizes the situation this way:

> "Miracles" and exorcisms are *a sign of the in-breaking of the kingdom of God*. In one sense, the kingdom has arrived in the person of Jesus; but in another sense, it is only *"near"* (Mark 1:15). Hence there is some ambiguity today about "miracles." They do occur, but they are to be *expected* only if the kingdom of God has *arrived*. It is, in fact, still *in the process of* arriving.[16]

Consequently, the descriptions of God's powerful presence and miraculous activity in modern Christian classics, such as Brother Andrew's *God's Smuggler*, David Wilkerson's *The Cross and the Switchblade*, and Jackie Pullinger's *Chasing the Dragon*, are quite credible. The specific situations described in those biographical accounts are in keeping with C. S. Lewis's astute observation: "Miracles [tend to occur in] areas *we* naturally have no wish to frequent."[17]

---

13. Ward, *Divine Action*, 182–83. Keith Ward also states, "Miracles . . . [are] astonishing and spiritually transforming signs of Divine presence, purpose, and power. God brings such miracles about by a special intention to enable creatures to come to a more conscious and dynamic relation with him" (ibid., 180).

14. Ibid., 180–81, 185.

15. Wright, *Jesus and the Victory of God*, 187.

16. Thiselton, *Systematic Theology*, 273, his emphasis.

17. Lewis, *Miracles*, 274, emphasis mine.

Part of the problem is one of connotation: a "kingdom" requires a king, and our automatic assumption is that God-as-king implies *omnipotence*, a rule of *power*. This is precisely the kind of Messiah the first-century Jews were expecting, and why they struggled to recognize Jesus' identity. We should not make the same mistake. As Good Friday shows, God's reign is *not* a rule of absolute power. God has addressed the problem of evil not through an overwhelming show of force—as we might expect or wish—but seemingly through the weakness and failure of Christ's crucifixion. The first Easter Saturday was, with the benefit of hindsight, an "in-between" time of waiting and wondering. While we live in this present age, we also wait for the age to come. We find this waiting hard; we wish the eschaton would come quickly. We long for that day when all that is wrong in the world will be finally put right. Like the first-century Christians, we don't understand the delay in the face of so much suffering. And we don't really understand why we don't see *more* glimpses of the future in the present. While we live with some frustration and impatience in the "now-and-not-yet" kingdom of God, there is also a sense of excitement and anticipation—for the best is yet to come.

The "Problem of Particularity"

At first glance it might seem that if God heals X but not Y then that is *unfair* and implies God has favorites. Even though Anne was not healed, I do not think this is the right way to approach the "problem of particularity." The reason why becomes obvious when we shine a light on the issue and its implications. If God healed everyone, or if God so arranged things such that no harm ever came to anyone, then this world would be unrecognizable to us. While that may be what we instinctively think a loving, all-powerful God *should* do, that is obviously not the way of God's providence. Nevertheless, the Christian view is that God can act in the world in extraordinary ways, and so—to put it crudely—it is better that such "mighty deeds" occur sometimes rather than not at all! That being the case, does God have a reason for acting in such ways when he does, and not at other times? Or in healing X but not Y? It seems most unlikely that a rational God does not have a reason and merely dispels acts of kindness randomly. But it is difficult to imagine what that reason might be.[18] However, just because God

---

18. Ward, *Divine Action*, 134.

heals an individual, does not mean that God *must* therefore heal everybody.[19] The above theology of miracles just presents a general framework, one that *only* allows us to place the particular in a broader context. Even in John's account of Jesus' healing at the pool of Bethsaida, only one man was healed when there were clearly many in need.[20]

The more we reflect on this matter, the more we realize that the idealized "God" proposed above would be totally impartial, uniform, and undifferentiated. This is just the opposite of the relational, responsive, and intimate Trinitarian God. As Keith Ward reminds us,

> The Christian God is above all a God of love, and as such he is bound to act to realize specific purposes for particular human persons. A love which is purely general, and exactly the same for everyone, is not real love, since it neglects precisely that uniqueness and particularity of the person which is the place of love to celebrate. . . . Real love is always active, responsive and particular.[21]

What this means is that although God loves each of us (John 3:16) and has no favorites (Acts 10:34; Rom 2:11), nevertheless the relationship the Trinity has with each of us is unique because *relationship necessitates our participation*. God wants us all to realize our full potential, to experience life in all its fullness. That is his heart's desire for each of us, but such a realization requires *our* cooperation and being in communion with God. The logic of this is obvious, even if it is not often articulated by ministers. The *relationship* God has with me is solely between God and me; the same is true for you—and for everyone else too. Each relationship with God is special and irreplaceable; it is to be treasured and nurtured. The problem of particularity is not really a "problem" as such, but simply a natural consequence of each person having their individual way of interrelating with the Trinity. It is important to add that this notion can—and *should*—be extended to communities, congregations, and society at large, rather than being restricted to a Western sense of individualism.

---

19. In a similar way, just because all the swans that you have observed are white does not mean that all swans are, or *must* be, white.

20. John 5:1–15.

21. Ward, *Divine Action*, 137–38. And John Polkinghorne writes, "Total impartiality would be total impersonality—which is not to say that a personal God has to have favourites, but that he will treat particular people in particular ways . . . without special providence, the idea of a personal God is emptied of content." Polkinghorne, *Science and Providence*, 48–49.

What this highlights is that the biblical God is not an impartial strategist, but is relational. God is therefore gracious and genuinely responds to an individual's (or a community's) prayer request. But God is not a magician performing tricks, nor someone whom we can manipulate. Since asking God to act "mightily" and compassionately in a given situation is a *petition*, one informed by our faith and relationship—however faltering—with the Divine, the outcome may not be what we earnestly desire. In which case we must *not* blame the victim or doubt the character/existence of God.[22] Instead, when we pray, we can pray with confidence knowing that our prayer is meaningful (i.e., not merely for psychological benefit) and has the *real* potential to alter the outcome of events.[23] We will explore this further in the next chapter.

Returning to our question: "If God heals X, why didn't God heal Y?" the usual first assumption is that God *could* have done so, because God is omnipotent. But as we have already seen in chapter 2, there are various theological and philosophical reasons why that traditional understanding of God's power must be qualified. From the very beginning of creation, God is a power-sharing deity, not a micromanager. As also mentioned earlier, the Creator endowed the cosmos (including humankind) with a significant degree of autonomy. This was discussed earlier in chapters 4 and 5 in the context of the free process defense. Second, we also assume the convoluted sets of circumstances are totally equivalent in both scenarios, and in our multifaceted world that is *never* the case. While God desires to heal both X and Y, *we* cannot know all the factors involved in the complex God-world relationship, and how they all interrelate in these two particular situations. What may be possible for X may not be possible for Y. At this point some may exclaim: "But the Bible says 'for God, *all* things are possible'!"[24] My response is to say: "Again, that viewpoint assumes a God of absolute omnipotence—and it doesn't mean everything is likely"! Those specific verses must be seen in the context of *salvation*, and Mary's acclamation in Luke 1:37 viewed in the context of Elizabeth's infertility. Mark's bold

22. Moreover, attaching conditions to a petition is a foolish attempt to corner, or test, God. The story of Gideon and his fleece (Judg 6:36–40) reflects God's graciousness in response to Gideon's faithlessness after witnessing ample reasons for faith (Judg 6:11–24). It is not to be emulated!

23. See also Ward, *Divine Action*, 154–69; Wilkinson, *When I Pray, What Does God Do?*; Reddish, *Science and Christianity*, 138–43.

24. See Matt 19:26; Mark 10:27; Luke 18:27. Note this is in response to the question, "Then who can be *saved*?" in the context of Jesus' encounter with the rich young man.

statements attributed to Jesus (Mark 9:23; 11:24) are, frankly, pastorally and experientially problematic.[25] If pastors are honest, they will admit these "promises"—taken at face value—create many more congregational problems than they solve! We are certainly encouraged *to* pray—to partner with God—and to pray with both confident faith in God's capabilities, and with a spirit of humility and forgiveness. Nevertheless, prayer is not a wizard's wand—as we all *know*![26] Yes, there is mystery—even tension—here, but I hope we can *trust* God to behave morally (i.e., not capriciously or arbitrarily) and to be true to his character, regardless of what transpires. In the final analysis, the precise details of what God is doing may be hidden from us, but that does not mean God is absent.

Finally, if—in response to the matter of particularity—our attitude is begrudging, then we have missed the theological point of miracles in the first place. A miracle is not a reward for good behavior and/or fervent faith! Moreover, concerning faith and doubt, some people agonize as to whether the "reason" they did not experience the miracle they so desperately sought was because they lacked sufficient faith. This mistakenly assumes that if you had *enough* faith, it would certainly tip the balance in your favor. I don't think God's providence functions like that! Miracles are not granted on the basis of a divine math formula, i.e., based on the magnitude of the faith-doubt ratio. Faith and doubt are inseparable—two sides of the same coin; the opposite of faith is *not* doubt, but certainty.[27] Mark relates an incident, following the Transfiguration, where the disciples could not heal a man's sick son—apparently due to the disciple's lack of faith and prayer.[28] It is impossible for us to know the faith-doubt ratio of the father in Mark 9:24 ("I believe, help my unbelief"), but *Jesus* had faith and responded graciously and compassionately in that situation; God was present. The father came to Jesus and was transparently honest with him. This act and attitude are *always* the right things to do. I can't help but wonder if the *quality* of the father's relationship with God, though important, had ultimately little to do with the final outcome. That, it seems to me, is a feature of *grace*.

25. "All things can be done for the one who believes," Mark 9:23; "So I tell you, whatever you ask for in prayer, believe that you have received it, and it will be yours," Mark 11:24. (See also Matt 21:21–22.)

26. I suggest this highlights the problem of proof-texting, and it forces us to seek a *broader* theological framework of the Trinity's activity in the world.

27. "We walk by faith, *not* by sight" (2 Cor 5:7). See also Heb 11:1.

28. See Mark 9:14–29.

Regardless of an inevitable element of mystery in such things, Christians believe God is *continually* active in all of creation and works to bring good out of evil. God engages people by his Spirit and partners with those who are cooperating with him and share and practice his values. And prayer and trust are key elements of that process.

Reasons for Hope

The way I presently see it is that God does not override human free will since that denies the freedom for a person to respond to God's love—for God cannot compel us to have faith. A consequence of this is that it is pointless to ask God in prayer for something that requires God to overrule the free will of another person. But I do not see that same issue with regard to physical, chemical, and biological processes, i.e., systems that do not have the capability to *respond* to God's love. A cancer cell, in my mind, cannot be lovingly "persuaded." God can, through the guise of random collisions, bring a chemotherapy drug into the vicinity of a cancer cell thereby allowing them to interact. Consequently, one can pray with confidence that God will bring about this possibility. This is a request for the treatment to be *effective* and is visualizing the *minimum* God can do![29] It is possible that complete healing will be the outcome. Despite such prayers for Anne, her cancer eventually metastasized and returned to other parts of her body. Further treatments occurred with similar prayers for their effectiveness. We cannot prove scientifically whether those prayers were efficacious, but I believe they were—resulting in a good quality of life for at least a year longer than had been expected.

In all this I have no definitive "answer," of course, but I have *hope*. Hope because of the reality of the resurrection, the character of the Trinitarian God, and because of my personal experience of God's presence along the unwanted path of suffering. In the end, we must also remember that dying is the ultimate healing for the Christian. Bishop James Jones writes, "The greatest gift that the risen Jesus Christ offers to our death-dreading world is not the secret of getting well but of dying well, in the sure and certain hope of the resurrection to eternal life."[30] Consequently, to pray for healing with a patient who has a terminal illness is perhaps better understood as

29. One can also pray for no postoperative infections or complications, and hence for a patient's speedy recovery.

30. Jones, *Why Do People Suffer?*, 98.

praying for more time to prepare everyone for what lies ahead. That is one reason a sudden death is so shocking. But the time prayed for is *quality* time, productive time, and for peace and mercy, not a pain-filled lingering. Jones also soberly reminds us,

> All the healings of Jesus were only temporary remissions. The people he healed and raised from the dead didn't live forever— they later died. This wasn't a failure on the part of Jesus. In healing people he wasn't saying that no one should ever fall ill and die.[31]

In conclusion, given that the Christ-event reveals the heart of the Trinity, we can know with confidence that God is at work bringing the world to right. While that will only be complete at the eschaton, we may witness "glimpses of the future in the present." Some of those miracles will involve the natural order—healings. Within a holistic worldview this is not problematic, as there is no differentiation between the physical and spiritual. Yet we also know God's world is a multifaceted matrix of interconnections, both in terms of people (all with free will) and in the intricate mesh of natural processes. Evidently, not everything is always possible. Anne was not healed. But this was not for lack of faith, nor because God did not *want* to heal her. (This is blaming the victim and doubting the character of God.) I don't find it helpful to apportion specific reasons, as this suggests a simple one-to-one correspondence in cause and effect.[32] I submit that, in this regard, the God-world relationship is more complicated than this correlation implies. This is, after all, what theodicy and theologies of divine action explore. As one who has experienced suffering, I find this comforting. Moreover, I know with confidence that God, Anne, and I—and all our prayerful supporters—were all working toward the same goal, namely for Anne's wholeness. We collaborated with God to do all we could to counter the evil of cancer. We worked with the medical profession to fight the

31. Ibid., 90–91.

32. There may be times when the correlation is well-established, as in the case of smoking and lung cancer; but no such connections were identified in Anne's situation. In addition, Gregory Boyd writes, "We don't know and can't know why particular harmful events unfold exactly as they do. What we *can* know, however, is *why* we can't know: it is not because God's plan or character is mysterious but because we are finite humans in an *incomprehensively vast creation* . . . The mystery of the particularity of evil is located in the mystery of creation, not the mystery of God. And given this mystery, we must refrain from blaming each other or blaming God when misfortunes arise." Boyd, *Is God to Blame?*, 102, his emphasis.

disease, as it is an integral part of God's healing activity in the world. These are positive, practical steps that all should take in such circumstances.

Seeing human suffering in this broader context does not *solve* anything—but that never should be the intent. What it does do, however, is create a faith-filled framework of hope. I also find it powerfully reassuring that even though we live in a world of pain and suffering, God is fundamentally opposed to evil and all its effects. The Trinity's definitive response to evil demonstrates a shouldering of the responsibility for creating this type of world where evil is possible. And it also speaks of Emmanuel—"God *with* us."

Courageous Faith

In Daniel 3 we read the inspirational story of Shadrach, Meshach, and Abednego and the fiery furnace. It is a remarkable tale of faith under pressure. These three Jewish officials in Nebuchadnezzar's kingdom refuse to bow down and worship his tall golden statue. Nebuchadnezzar is furious when he hears of their snub to his gods, but gives them one more chance to prove their allegiance and, if they still are obstinate, he threatens,

> You will be immediately thrown into a blazing furnace. Then what god will be able to rescue you from my hand?[33]

It is the bold response of the three men that is so impressive:

> If we are thrown into the blazing furnace, the God we serve is able to deliver us from it, and he will deliver us from Your Majesty's hand. *But even if he does not*, we want you to know, Your Majesty, that we will not serve your gods or worship the image of gold you have set up.[34]

Now *that's* a principled stance based on their faith in God! They know that God has delivered his people from oppression in the past—indeed the exodus from Egypt is the defining moment for the young Jewish nation. So they therefore know that God is capable of delivering them from certain death. However, *they* are not going to instigate a showdown between the one true God and Nebuchadnezzar's gods. They will serve God *regardless*

33. Dan 3:15b.
34. Dan 3:17–18, emphasis mine.

of the consequences and, if they perish, the king should not regard that outcome as vindication. Truly amazing courage!

What happens next? The king is extremely angry; he orders the fire to be superhot and for his strongest soldiers to tie them up. The furnace was so hot that soldiers died as they threw Shadrach, Meshach, and Abednego into the fire! The king then leaps to his feet in amazement:

> Weren't there three men that we tied up and threw into the fire?
> . . . Look, I see four men walking around the fire, unbound and unharmed, and the fourth looks like a son of the gods.[35]

King Nebuchadnezzar orders them to come out of the fire, acknowledges the one true God and even promotes the three young men.

In this great drama of deliverance and faith, we note that the fourth person is identified by Nebuchadnezzar as a divine being, an angel (3:28), who is alongside them in their suffering. Even the unbelieving king recognized the significance of this sign and responded with a U-turn: repentance.

While this is a story of faith under religious persecution, which is not exactly the same as everyday physical suffering, the attitude of the three Jewish officials is, I believe, worthy of emulation. As they affirmed: God certainly has delivered his people from suffering in the past; but it is inappropriate to *demand* a miracle. Regardless of the outcome of our prayers, we will continue to serve and honor the living God. And we can be assured that God identifies with those who suffer and comes along side us, if we would but recognize him, even "freeing" us within the situation itself.

Now *that's* courageous faith!

35. Dan 3:24–25.

8

Co-prayer with the Spirit

To be a Christian without prayer is no more possible
than to be alive without breathing.

—MARTIN LUTHER

Prayer is the most concrete way to make our home in God.

—HENRI NOUWEN

Introduction

Matthew tells us that Jesus taught his followers to ask for God's "will to be done on earth, as it is in Heaven."[1] We repeat this phrase all the time in the Lord's Prayer to the point that we have forgotten what the words imply. That statement says we should continue to pray for God's kingdom to be established, because what we see here and now is *not* all that God desires. God does *not* always get what God wants. Moreover, our prayers are, it seems, needed to help bring about God's rule—his kingdom—here on earth. In fact, more than our prayers

---

1. Matt 6:10.

are needed. We also need to *act*—to be empowered by the Spirit and work to bring about the things God values. Saying "your will be done on earth as it is in heaven" is, then, not merely an expression of eschatological hope—although it is that—but it is an affirmation of our commitment to partner with our Trinitarian God to further God's kingdom.[2]

Yet many wonder what *actually* happens when we pray, and ask what can and will God *do* in response to our prayers?[3] This is an important pastoral issue, particularly in the face of suffering. If we could better understand the process and potency of prayer, we would be more inclined to pray. Following on from the previous chapter, this chapter further explores some aspects of the mysterious deep waters of prayer. It builds on earlier chapters where we addressed the character of God and the nature of the world God created and continually sustains. We will focus here on one facet of the Holy Spirit's role in prayer, one that Christians often overlook, by studying (in some detail) Romans 8:26–27. Furthermore, since prayer is practical, I will also share personal insights concerning prayer as Anne and I journeyed with cancer. Naturally, the tone in that "Question and Answer" section will become pastoral, as is appropriate.

Physicist-theologian John Polkinghorne gives two criteria for theological coherence in prayer.[4] The first is simply that prayer only makes sense in *a certain kind of world*. Prayer is illogical in the rigid framework of a purely clockwork universe. Although—as mentioned in the previous chapter—modern physics insists that our world is *not* closed like that, the legacy of that Newtonian paradigm lingers in our consciousness. That mechanistic worldview is officially dead; let us not resurrect it within our *theology* and so inhibit our view of God's capabilities and activities in the world. Instead, let us embrace a world that is open to new and emergent possibilities. Second, prayer only makes sense with *a certain kind of God*. God needs to be relational, engaged with time—our experience of sequential events—rather than purely "outside" of time. With these two in place, Polkinghorne concludes prayer is not a "nonsensical idea" but becomes a "rational possibility."[5] Only from this perspective of openness and relationality will we have the confidence to engage in the discipline of prayer.

2. See also Boring, "Matthew," 203–4.

3. See also Wilkinson, *When I Pray, What Does God Do?*

4. Polkinghorne *Science and Providence*, 84.

5. Ibid. John Polkinghorne also writes, "The picture we have is . . . that of a world of regularity but not rigidity, within whose evolving history there is room for action

Nevertheless, prayer is not a magical incantation, and it cannot change the facts of the present situation—just like the past cannot be altered. Neither can a prayer's effectiveness be proved or disproved logically. Just because a specific request was "granted" does not mean that the outcome would *not* have been realized had we *not* prayed. We are bound by the arrow of time; we cannot go back and run through the exact same scenario again, this time without prayer, and see if the same result is achieved. We need not, unless we choose to, believe in the causal connection between the prayer and result. The effectiveness of prayer, like the significance of miracles, is a matter of faith. Consequently, prayer is a living expression of our relationship with God and his commitment to us.

How God will respond to our requests we cannot say, since *we* do not know the constraints of the whole system or the involvement of others—not forgetting that they too have free will. Nevertheless in the complex web of possibilities within an open world, our prayer may enable God to shift the constraints in a favorable direction to respond to our prayer.[6] Since our prayers become part of the causal matrix, prayer will *always* make a difference to the world—even if it does not expressly give us the outcome we desire.[7]

While I—as a scientist—value this logic and find that it encourages me to pray, I can appreciate that for others this rationale may seem cold, perhaps even disturbing! Regardless, and as I mentioned before, we need to have confidence in the effectiveness of prayer if we are to practice it. And, as Luther and Nouwen remind us at the beginning of this chapter, the more

---

initiated both by human will (which we experience directly) and by divine will (which we acknowledge by faith). There must be a delicate balance between structure and flexibility, between the respect for cosmic freedom (which delivers physical processes from arbitrary interruption) and the respect for human freedom (which allows us the exercise of choice and responsibility) and the respect for divine freedom (which does not reduce God to the role of an impotent spectator in the history of his creation). It is an immensely difficult task, beyond our powers to accomplish in any detail, to see how this works out, but I claim that the insights of science, and in particular the death of mere mechanism, are consonant with this view" (ibid., 81–82).

6. Ward, *Divine Action*, 163.

7. Ibid., 169. Gregory Boyd expresses it this way: "Prayer makes a difference, but so do the necessary regularity of the world and every free choice humans and angels make. We have no way of knowing how the power of prayer intersects with these and other variables. We can pray with confidence, knowing our prayer is heard and makes a difference. But we can't pray with certainty that the difference our prayer makes will have the precise outcome we desire. In this sense we can't be certain our prayer will be answered." Boyd, *Is God to Blame?*, 134.

we engage with God in prayer, the more it becomes second nature, i.e., dynamic evidence of our relationship with God.

The Holy Spirit and Intercessory Prayer

A Trinitarian formula for prayer is that we "pray *through* the Son *to* the Father *in* the Spirit." What does this mean? Praying "through the Son" is based on Jewish imagery and refers to Jesus acting in a High Priestly role as our intermediary (e.g., Heb 4:14–16). But what does it mean to "pray in the Spirit," particularly in the context of suffering? Romans 8:22–27 is helpful in this regard.[8] As will become evident, it presents a radical way to view prayer:

> We know that the whole creation has been groaning in labor pains until now; and not only the creation, but we ourselves, who have the first fruits of the Spirit, groan inwardly while we wait for adoption, the redemption of our bodies. For in hope we were saved. Now hope that is seen is not hope. For who hopes for what is seen? But if we hope for what we do not see, we wait for it with patience. *Likewise the Spirit helps us in our weakness; for we do not know how to pray as we ought, but that very Spirit intercedes with sighs too deep for words. And God, who searches the heart, knows what is the mind of the Spirit, because the Spirit intercedes for the saints according to the will of God.*[9]

Remarkably, perhaps, the above well-known text is the only reference within Scripture to the Spirit interceding *for us*. One key aspect of its uniqueness is that the Spirit, who traditionally was *sent* by the Father, is—in this situation—explicitly communicating *to* the Father.[10] These verses provide a powerful—and often overlooked—rationale for prayer, especially in light of the doctrine of the Trinity. Prayer is never done in isolation, but is *co-prayer* with the Spirit.

One word from 8:26 that has been much debated is that of "weakness." What does this mean in this context, given Paul's confident exhortation in

---

8. Note too Eph 6:18: "Pray *in the Spirit* at all times in every prayer and supplication." See also Jude 20.

9. Rom 8:22–27, emphasis mine.

10. This role is consistent with that of an "advocate" (*paraclete*); but even in the Fourth Gospel, the author's usage of that term has the Spirit's work directed *toward* humankind rather than oriented to the Father (see John 14:16, 26; 15:26; 16:7).

Philippians 4:6?[11] Since Paul included himself in this category, it is more likely a not knowing *what* (NIV) to pray, rather than *how* (NRSV) to pray—and this is consistent with the following verse. This being the case, our weakness is being at a loss to know what to ask for in prayer, especially if we do not know the will (or mind) of God on a particular matter—or if hope is fading (8:24–25). Alternatively, we know what we want to ask, but our desires may not be aligned with those of God. Either way, the Spirit comes to our aid.

But there is more to it than that. Paul has a broader theme, together with link words/clauses (e.g., "likewise"), within Romans 8.[12] He stresses that the certain future glory outweighs our present sufferings (8:17–18), followed by the triplet of groanings (the longing creation, the hoping Christian, and the interceding Spirit; 8:22, 23, 26). The use of the word "weakness" in this context is a reference to our present state of not yet being *fully* redeemed, i.e., an inaugurated eschatology—the "now-and-not-yet" reign of God.[13] Robert Jewett expresses the same sentiment: "Our weakness refers to the believer's vulnerable position of being caught between two ages, knowing enough of the coming age to yearn for it (along with the rest of creation) but continuing to be assaulted by the principalities and powers of the old age of the flesh."[14]

The key point, however, is that the "very Spirit" (8:26)—not an angel—helps us in our weakness. The one who is active on the behalf of the Christian is the same Spirit who dwells in the believer (8:9–11)—the same Spirit that enables us to cry out *Abba* Father" (8:15). Moreover, the Greek word for "helps" is strong, as in "concrete aid," or the one who actively takes the brunt of the load that we cannot carry alone. While the Spirit does not take over the Christian's responsibility to pray, the Spirit is always ready to come to our assistance. This is comforting news, especially in the context of suffering. The Christian *never* prays alone.

11. "Do not worry about anything, but in everything by prayer and supplication with thanksgiving let your requests be made known to God."

12. Care is needed when leaping into Paul's complex argument and rhetoric in this epistle. Only a few verses later, Paul adds (in a different context) that "it is Christ Jesus, who died, yes, who was raised, who is at the right hand of God, who indeed *intercedes* for us" (Rom 8:34; see also the heaven court imagery of 2:1–16).

13. See Wright, "Letter to the Romans," 598.

14. Jewett, *Romans*, 522.

The triple use of the word "sighs" or "groans" is curious. An obvious parallel is the groans of the Israelites in slavery in Egypt (Exod 2:24; 6:5),[15] and Tob 3:1 expresses a sentiment that is in keeping with that of Paul: "Then with much grief and anguish of heart I wept, and with groaning began to pray." Some might say that the Spirit assists and makes up for any lacking in our earnestness; but that can only be part of the story. Some scholars have taken the Spirit's inexpressible groanings to mean "speaking in tongues." However, this seems most unlikely as the Greek words Paul uses imply "speechless" or "voiceless."[16] Neither does this mean silent prayer or contemplation, since in Paul's day most people would read—and pray—aloud even when alone.[17] Instead, these prayers seem to be agonizing laments that are too heartfelt to be articulated. The groans convey a sense of intensity and sincerity. They represent a profound yearning and a deep desire for the request to be heard and addressed. Interestingly, Paul seems to expect his audience to understand this experience—just as he does when he uses the expression "*Abba* Father" (8:15). N. T. Wright puts it this way:

> The Spirit's own very self intercedes with the Christian at precisely the point where he or she, faced with the ruin and misery of the world, find there are no words left to express in God's presence the sense of futility (8:20) and longing for redemption. . . . The Spirit active within the innermost being of the Christian, is doing the very interceding the Christian longs to do, even though the only evidence that can be produced is inarticulate groaning.[18]

You might ask, "How precisely does the Spirit intercede?" Does the Spirit cry out *directly* on our behalf, or *indirectly* by stirring up in our hearts those desires which are appropriate? John Calvin favored the latter.[19] This implies the indwelling Spirit not only knows heart of God, but also intimately knows the believer's heart (see also 1 Cor 2:10). Moreover, the Spirit intercedes indirectly by helping believers to communicate with God through the *believers'* prayers and groans. However plausible that sounds, the Greek and the overall context imply *directly*. Some—because of their prior commitment to divine impassivity—will then object: "God's Spirit

15. Note: this same Greek word is used in Exod 2:24; 6:5 in the LXX translation of the Hebrew Scriptures.

16. Wright, "Letter to the Romans," 599; Fitzmyer, *Romans*, 519.

17. Wright, "Letter to the Romans," 599.

18. Ibid.

19. Calvin, *Commentary on Romans*, 272.

can't groan!" But we have already seen in chapter 2, that strict adherence to divine impassivity and immutability is unsustainable. Consequently, I—like many others—would disagree: prayer not only changes things, prayer also changes *God*.

In 8:27 the Father is referred to as "the Heart Searcher." Recall that in Hebraic thought the heart is the center of "being," the source of will, emotion, and intentionality.[20] Concerning God as the Heart Searcher, Origen states, "Paul shows here that God pays less attention to the words we use in prayer than he does to what is in our heart and mind."[21] However, the context here is in searching the heart *of the Spirit*, who is intimately dwelling within the saints (8:9–11, 14–16), as well as being an integral person within the Trinity.[22] Whatever our own groanings may mean (8:23), the Spirit's groaning (8:26) is not only comprehended by the Heart Searcher, but is inevitably in accordance with the will of God (8:27). For Christians who are waiting in patience and living in hope (8:25), this is a bold affirmation as to the effectiveness of prayer. It is in this context, then, that Paul continues,

> We know that all things work together for good for those who love God. . . . What then are we to say about these things? If God is for us, who is against us?[23]

Wright suggests Paul's rationale should be understood as:

> God knows the mind of the Spirit; *but* we know that God works all things together for good for those who love God; therefore (implicit but vital) God works all things together for good for us, we in whom the Spirit is operating. . . . "All things"—not just the groanings of the previous verses, but the entire range of experiences and events that may face God's people—are taken care of by the creator God who is planning to renew the whole creation, and us along with it.[24]

---

20. Jewett, *Romans*, 524.

21. Bray, *Romans*, 231.

22. It is important to note that this Trinitarian inference is from *later* theology, rather than explicitly from within this text. From a Trinitarian perspective, the Spirit need not utter anything, as the Father knows the Spirit's intention without it being expressed. This reminds us that contemporary Christians read Scripture through a Trinitarian lens and, consequently, not everything is neat and tidy.

23. Rom 8:28a, 31.

24. Wright, "Letter to the Romans," 600.

The believer, then, has *two* intercessors: Jesus who intercedes in heaven at the right hand of the Father (8:34), and the Spirit who intercedes while resident within believers.[25] These are not two rival intercessors, of course, since the ultimate aim of both the Spirit and the Son is to bring the believer into the Father's fellowship! However, though it might be tempting to simply equate the intercessory actions of Christ with those of the Spirit in this passage, their *locations* force us to maintain the differentiation. All this provides motivation to exercise the spiritual discipline of prayer, which Calvin describes as the perpetual (or chief) exercise of faith.[26]

In summary, it is quite legitimate to state that the believer and the Spirit are "co-praying." As Daniel Migliore says, "Prayer is the fundamental exercise of the new human freedom in *partnership* with the Spirit of God."[27] Since our prayers are in partnership with the Spirit, who is intimately involved in the divine dance with the Father and the Son, then this further adds significant potency to our prayers. In which case, this is indeed a revolutionary approach to prayer and provides further powerful incentive for the believer to pray. And to pray with confidence that our prayers are not only heard, but they matter—and they make a real difference in the world.

Pastoral and Personal Perspectives on Prayer in the Context of Suffering

Our church traveled with Anne and me as we walked on our journey with cancer. It raised many questions that our minister, Mary, needed to address. I responded to some of the issues myself, both before and after Anne died. The questions below arose from conversations with Mary, the concerns of close friends and the wider congregation, and from my personal reflection.

>   *1. A great deal of prayer was made for Anne, at church and from friends and family around the world. People prayed fervently for complete healing and yet she wasn't. Why do you think that God didn't heal Anne?*

As discussed in the previous chapter, I have no definitive answer to that question and it is not something that preys on my mind.[28] However, I do

---

25. Joseph Fitzmyer regards the Spirit as the source of *all* genuine Christian prayer, not just petition (*Romans*, 518).

26. Calvin, *Institutes*, bk. 3, ch. 20, 682.

27. Migliore, *Faith Seeking Understanding*, 242; emphasis mine.

28. We can *never* know the answers to such specific questions! But the question is

passionately believe that God *wanted* to heal Anne. I believe that God loved Anne and was very sad about her steady decline in health; her untimely death was not what God wanted to happen (i.e., deliberately planned). So the reason why Anne was not healed is not, at least in my mind, located in the heart of God, and because of that, I am not angry with God. Furthermore, I do not think that it was because of a "lack of faith." Sometimes such phrases are thrown around in either implied or explicit accusation. Like the unhelpful words of Job's comforters, this phrase can be hurtful; I just don't believe it to be true for Anne. There *was* faith, we had faith and there were plenty of people praying. Some of those people were champions of prayer and others were new Christians who simply wanted God to bless Anne. To be honest, I am not sure to which of those two categories of people God pays more attention; oftentimes I think it is the latter! But they all combine to provide a matrix of prayer to the Heart Searcher.

So if the problem is not located in the heart of God or in the faith of individuals praying, then there is no need to point fingers, which would be counterproductive. In addition, in this—and every—situation we have at least three other factors: a very complex world, a specific disease, and an individualized body chemistry. So perhaps it was simply not possible to have *complete* healing for Anne. There could have been some partial healing or protection within her physical body. No one will ever know for sure, and such things can only be interpreted through the eyes of faith. For instance, amazingly, Anne's cancer in her neck remained stable for five years. She had full mobility and walked on the treadmill most days for about forty-five minutes. Given the seriousness of the situation, being confined to a wheelchair had been a possible outcome. Anne also responded to other treatments, and her liver cancer decreased and remained under control throughout her life. I thank God for that. Of course we made full use of the treatment options available to us. In doing so we believed we were giving God options—more windows of opportunity—and so further advancing the possibility of God healing Anne.

As an aside, I confess I find it a bit irksome when I hear of people refusing medical opportunities (surgeries, treatments) openly available to them because they fervently believe that God will heal them "supernaturally" without medical intervention. On one hand I admire their faith and perhaps God sometimes honors it, but in general I feel God is shouting,

---

asked out of a desire to understand a broader framework of God's activity in the context of personal suffering; this is my response.

"Come on, help me out here and meet me half way!" All healing comes from God and we should make full use of medical expertise that is open to us. As I see it, our faith, everyone's prayers, and Anne's willingness and determination to undergo all the treatments made available to her, were our side of the divine partnership.

2. *With your partnership model, and with hindsight, was there more that should have been done—things that perhaps could have "enabled" God to do more?*

This is another good—yet impossible—question to answer, but one that is particularly relevant in a pastoral situation; in other words, what can we learn from this for the future? Personally, it is not something that troubles me or gives me any cause for regret—I will explain why in a moment. I would certainly want to repeat all that we did for Anne as a church for someone else in similar circumstances: the individual prayer, the group prayer, anointing with oil, support group, etc.

Perhaps it would be worth exploring further the role of fasting in such situations. It seems to me that this spiritual discipline is not something we talk about much in the Western Church today, and, indeed, I have not studied the topic and I have no firm "theology of fasting"! One potential issue with such self-sacrificial acts is our motivation. In fasting for a period of time, we are *not*—I hope—trying to manipulate God or twist his arm—as if we could! Such an attitude is built on the fearful premise that we need to somehow beg God to be on *our* side and so *persuade* God to act accordingly. This isn't Trinitarian thinking, is it? It is ridiculous to imagine that healing is, even partially, a matter of a "correct recipe" of spiritual acts that need to be performed in order to get the desired result. More to the point, such an attitude is not in the spirit of *partnership* and it fails to grasp that the God of grace and love is always alongside his followers, and those who seek him. But, if we are *authentically* partnering with God, then—it seems to me—the sacrificial act of fasting, like prayer, will always have some beneficial impact in the world in ways that we cannot truly understand.

Having said that, I remain convinced that even *if* had we "prayed *and* fasted," the outcome would have been the same in our particular situation. Why? Because God knew the *hearts* of all those who were praying for Anne; God knew of the sincerity, as well as the honest doubt. Not only were *we* partnering with God, but the suffering Trinitarian God was partnering with *us*. Therefore, I am convinced that if God really thought that fasting would be a critical or, potentially, the deciding factor in healing Anne, then

I am sure God would have communicated that to us. I know that, among the many who prayed, there are those with spiritual discernment. I am confident that God would have brought the urgency of fasting to their (and our) attention, if this would have been helpful. God—the Heart Searcher—is gracious.

> 3. *How do you feel now when prayer requests arise relating to others who are battling with cancer and requiring God's healing?*

I have a special affinity for such prayer requests and, naturally, I pray for God to completely heal them. I pray for the wisdom of the surgeons, that their hands may be God's agents of healing. I pray for the oncologists, and for the chemotherapy treatment—that as those chemicals cruise around the body they will reach and kill every cancer cell. I pray that God will multiply the expected effectiveness of those drugs in dealing with cancer. I pray for similar microscopic effectiveness in radiation treatments too. I pray for the "maximum effectiveness with the minimum of side effects." We prayed this for Anne and, of course, I pray it for others. I want God to be involved in any healing possible. I also want God to remove any fear and to bring peace. I pray that those suffering will know in a real and personal way that the living Jesus is walking right beside them; that "God is here, his Spirit is with us," and that they will know this is true regardless of the outcome. Each person is different; each cancer case is different, the physical and spiritual circumstances are also different. It seems to me that what was not possible in the case of Anne may still be possible in another situation and therefore I pray that God will be able to do *all* that is possible for them in their *unique* set of circumstances. Indeed it is because each situation is truly unique that we should continue to humbly ask God for full healing.

> 4. *When you realized that full healing wasn't going to happen, did you stop praying for that?*

Certainly in the first two years it was appropriate to pray for *complete* healing. But once the cancer returned, in this case to Anne's spine and, most critically, to her neck, we had to review the situation. Prayer is a conversation and therefore what is God "saying" when the disease spreads? Of course we continued to pray for the effectiveness of treatments, but it seemed natural to assume that *complete* healing was now, while not impossible, significantly less likely to happen. There came a point much later on when I started to pray that God would ensure Anne's dying would be merciful and peaceful. That may seem to some like a terrible thing for which to pray; indeed it may seem to imply a shocking "lack of faith." However, in real situations it is important to pray for the realistic. I hasten to add that there was no sense of resignation within Anne (or myself) to the disease; she was a fighter whatever the prognosis and I am sure God never "gave up" either—he was *continually* at work. I'm convinced that God was able to fully answer that prayer for mercy, and I am so thankful to him for doing so.

5. *Did you feel God was with you, or did it seem like the shout of silence?*

From the very beginning Anne and I had a special sense of God being with us, of Emmanuel, of Jesus walking alongside us day by day. Christ was with us and gave us hope, strength, peace, and a quiet assurance of his love as we walked on this unwanted journey of suffering together. I can't *explain* it rationally, I just think it has been one of those profound gifts that God gave us, which neither of us expected at the outset and one which, despite the sadness that we felt, resulted in us having no major crises or crippling fear. Christians trot out the biblical phrase "the peace that passes under-standing" (Phil 4:7) all too glibly. Perhaps I can paraphrase and amplify it: "having a quiet, calm awareness of God's peace and presence in a way that defies all logic in the circumstances." Of course we were not saints or perfect in that situation! Nor were we stoics; we were human. It hurt, we wept, and we quietly mourned the loss of our future relationship together. But somehow we knew that it was not just two of us on this walk, but three; Jesus himself shared with us in the good times, the funny times, as well as the very sad times. This, to me, was the most important aspect of our journey. This was aided by close friends, God's agents, walking along side us and supporting us in wonderful ways, such that we will never be able to truly express our gratitude. Thank God for his family, the church; when it functions well, it is awesome.

6. *Were there times that you felt God was particularly close to you?*

Christians celebrate Holy Communion in a variety of ways. For some the eating of the bread and the drinking of the wine are simply symbolic acts of remembrance; for others, those acts are far more profound—Com-munion is a sacrament. I am one of the latter and therefore, to me, Christ's presence can be experienced in a mystical way, that is nevertheless acutely real, during Communion. It is a faith position; I can't prove it. But my ex-pectation of experiencing God in a special, intimate way is heightened at such times. Our minister frequently reminded us of this sacramental aspect and that the Holy Spirit often works in unexpected, yet loving and positive, ways as we receive of "the gifts of God, for the people of God."

On one such occasion, after returning to my pew having just received the bread and wine, I acknowledged in prayer that the same power that had *raised Jesus from the dead* was now mystically *embodied* within Anne and me.[29] The risen Christ was not just *with* us, but *in* us. It is a formidable thought. At that moment, I suddenly felt warm, as if I had been wrapped in a hot blanket. I interpret this as a sign that the Holy Spirit was pouring healing, hope, courage, and peace into the core of my being. Some who read these words may find it weird and emotional; others will recognize it for what it is: a gracious anointing.

This special moment didn't last long; in my experience such occasions never do. Although God *may* have been doing some physical healing in Anne at that time, I did not *claim* this experience as a sign of miraculous activity. It was, for me, a quiet but vivid reassurance of God's presence in our situation. It was a confirmation, if one were needed, that God was on the case; he was powerfully at work.

29. Since, in marriage, "the two become one," I have no problem in envisioning my wife and me as a unit!

9

A Time to Cry, a Time to Wait, a Time to Celebrate

Blessed are those who mourn, for they will be comforted.

—MATTHEW 5:4

Come to me, all you that are weary and are carrying heavy burdens, and I will give you rest.

—MATTHEW 11:28

No eye has seen, nor ear heard, nor the human heart conceived, what God has prepared for those who love him.

—1 CORINTHIANS 2:9

Letting Go

Over what would turn out to be Anne's last few months, we could sense that her memory was getting gradually worse, as was her struggle to find certain words. She was also more unsteady on her feet and found stairs increasingly difficult. Anne very reluctantly agreed to give up her daily walk on the treadmill "for a while." She religiously maintained her daily cocktail of pills, creams, and injections, but now she needed some prompting and everything took more time. Her daily afternoon naps lasted longer. I responded by spending as much time as I could working from home.

Anne loved baking and cooking; it gave her much pleasure. I knew her condition was deteriorating when one day, after her nap, she wanted to make a nice meal and got out various ingredients and a recipe. I left her to it and worked for an hour in my study. On returning to the kitchen, thinking the meal would have been well underway by then, I found Anne struggling to comprehend the recipe and was looking with bewilderment at some weighed-out ingredients in front of her, unsure what to do next. So we made the meal together. This was so unlike Anne, and I realized her brain tumors were progressing, despite the second dose of radiation.

The day after Christmas, which was a happy family affair (and a full Christmas dinner!), we spent the night in the Emergency Room while Anne had fluid drained from her lungs. This was a new development. A few weeks later the oncologist and palliative care team wanted to keep Anne in the hospital "overnight" to properly assess her condition, and to modify and monitor her medications. The oncologist said to me softly, "I am sure she must be experiencing more pain than she admits." I reflected on that; I honestly don't think that this was the case. Anne, I am sure, had a high pain tolerance, but she certainly wasn't heroic about it! I just don't think that she was *aware* of the pain the oncologist was expecting. I still wonder if that was simply part of God's gracious gift of mercy to Anne. I suspect it was.

For Anne to be in hospital was the best place for her at that time and, understandably, was a welcome relief for me as her caregiver. The overnight stay initially lasted a weekend, by which time Anne perked up due to the new medications. But this was, not unpredictably, short-lived relief. What was initially anticipated to be a brief stay in the hospital turned out to be her last visit. Events moved rapidly during the following week, yet throughout that time Anne remained herself. She smiled, was cheerful, and was remarkably brave. Of course there were tears too; tears of loss for what might have been.

On the Monday, two musicians came into Anne's hospital room (while I was not there) and played and sang "Amazing Grace" to her, which she found powerful. A day or so later, two close friends and I were sitting in her room chatting when we heard the sound of singing in the corridor. We strained to hear what song it was and we slowly realized, from the tune, that it was the traditional hymn "What a Friend We Have in Jesus," but sung in a different language. "I know who that is," exclaimed Anne. "It's those people who sang 'Amazing Grace' the other day—quick think of a hymn they can sing when they come here." We were much less enthusiastic about this idea; our friends suggested we close the door or fake being asleep! Anne was having none of that, "Think of a suitable song," she insisted. After a prolonged pause, someone asked, "Must it be religious?" We figured probably not. "I know," exclaimed Anne. "How about 'Live and Let Die,'" and loudly hummed the subsequent dramatic chords of Paul McCartney's theme song to her favorite Bond movie. We all fell about laughing, but Anne was serious. I politely pointed out that such a song may not be the most appropriate one for an oncology ward! It turned out to be simply a visiting group to a neighboring patient, so, thankfully, we were let off the hook. But this illustrates Anne's spirit, which infected us all. While aware of the sadness and uncertainty of exactly what lay ahead, there was a sense of peace in her room.

On Friday, Anne was medically in a very different place. Her condition was changing quickly and the medical team was rapidly adjusting and responding to her needs. For a short time Anne appeared mildly agitated in what was a probably involuntary muscular movement of her arms; we were, of course, saying loving, calming, and reassuring words to Anne. Rita, our amazing pain specialist, quietly brought in the same two musicians who happened to be in the ward at that time. They again played and sang "Amazing Grace." Ruth—another close friend from church—and I were present with Anne at that moment; it was *we* who were moved to tears, which we bravely—but hopelessly—tried to suppress. Music can penetrate your heart when you least expect it. We consequently sang Chris Tomlin's version of "Amazing Grace" at the funeral.[1]

In addition to Anne's friends visiting her, hearing and watching DVDs of *Live* concerts of Simply Red, Dido, and David Gilmour, there are a host

---

1. Chris Tomlin's modern adaptation of John Newton's classic hymn is entitled "My Chains Are Gone." See http://wordtoworship.com/song/130.

of other memorable, moving, and sometimes funny events that happened during that week. I related some during the funeral service, as you will see below. Without being "super-spiritual" or clichéd, *God's presence was also there*. He was there in the excellent health care given by the nurses and doctors. He was there in the steadfast love and support of friends who stood vigil with us day and night. But I think the evidence of God's presence was *more* than simply within those individuals. He was there, among our sadness, with a special sense of peace and mercy. Moreover, God's mystical presence was not fleeting but continual—at times intense. He had not abandoned us and there was no sense of fear or despair. For those of us who were there, well, we will not forget that time as long as we live. Perhaps God even sent angels to meet his beloved daughter, Anne, to welcome her into his presence. Why should Christians, of all people, be surprised by that?

I have no idea how one actually feels as one personally faces death. Who of us can know? I know Anne wanted to continue living life to the full and experience all the things one generally regards as "normal." This is, of course, appropriate for any one facing an untimely death. And so Anne fought to live, rather than being eager to be with Christ. Yet I wonder what crossed her mind during those final days while being surrounded by those she loved and those who loved her? Anne must have understood that her "race" (2 Tim 4:7) here was nearly over, and what was to come would be indescribably better. I found this quote by Malcolm Muggeridge powerful and moving. He expresses, in his own style, the joy of what is and of what is to come. Perhaps similar things crossed Anne's mind:

> I am an old man, already passed the allotted three score and ten years and, as the old do, I quite often wake up in the night, half out of my body, so that I see between the sheets the old battered carcass I shall soon be leaving for good, and in the distance a glow in the sky, the lights of Augustine's City of God. Let me pass on two extraordinarily sharp impressions which accompany this condition. The first is of the incredible beauty of our earth, its colors and shapes and smells and creatures; of the enchantment of human love and companionship, of the fulfilment of human work and human procreation. The second, a certainty surpassing all words and thought, that as an infinitesimal particle of God's creation I am a participant in His purposes, which are loving, not malign, creative not destructive, orderly not chaotic—and in that certainty a great peace and a great joy.[2]

2. Hunter, *Best of Malcolm Muggeridge*, 263.

136

Flying to the Catcher

At Anne's funeral service I read the following tribute. In doing so I was deliberately sharing with our church and friends some of what occurred in private during Anne's last week. To some extent our church was in shock. On one Sunday people were praying for Anne at church and were told she was in hospital having a medical "tune-up." The following Sunday the congregation were sadly informed that Anne had died an hour and a half earlier.

It has been an exhausting two weeks for me, with each day bringing changes to Anne's condition which, understandably, meant that my heart and mind could barely keep up with the pace of events. However, I would like to relate two of what will be my abiding personal memories of her last week.

Our son, Philip, and his wife, Greer, phoned Anne in hospital every day from Halifax (Nova Scotia). You could see her face light up as she heard their voices, and I recall her excited determination and struggle as she tried to talk back to them. Later, they managed to dodge a severe winter storm in Halifax and arrived last Friday at lunchtime. Anne's *radiance* on her face will always be etched on my mind, as she knew that her son was there with her, face-to-face. Later that evening Anne was in a peaceful unconscious state; silent, but with her strong heart beating on.

I would now like to relate our experience of Sunday morning, the moments surrounding Anne's dying. The nurse came in to check on Anne and kindly suggested that it would be better if the room was quieter—not that we were noisy! So we discussed just having one person with Anne and the others being outside. Greer, who happens to be a cardiac ICU nurse, bravely told her father-in-law that *I* was the problem—and that I needed to leave the room and give Anne "space." Over the previous two days I had whispered reassurance in Anne's ear that I would be well looked-after, as would be Philip and her elderly father, Ernest. I was trying to release her and so let her know she was free to go. That my being there might be counterproductive was a surprise to me, as I so wanted to be present for her. It had not occurred to me that Anne might be determined, subconsciously, to protect me from witnessing her moment of dying. As if to confirm Greer's insight, Anne's breathing changed suddenly and slowed down. We all looked at each other for a moment, as we thought she had died right then. But the slow erratic pace of her breathing continued. I took my cue and left the room, and went to the washroom. On returning, the

137

others were in the hallway, making me think it was now all over, but Mary said that they were giving Anne time alone. I sat down on a chair in the hall and wept, knowing that Anne would likely soon die. As Mary came to comfort me, Greer went back into the room to check on Anne. This coming and going was all in a matter of minutes.

Unknown to us, Andrew Templer had been reading his Bible earlier that morning, as is his faithful daily discipline. A verse from a psalm "leapt out of the page" at him as being especially relevant for me. I should add—as those who know Andrew well will already appreciate—he does not make a habit of such claims! He then went out to walk the dog, Henry, and later called the hospital to pass on his verse to me.

The precise sequence of what happened next, and who knew what when, is a bit of a blur. Unbeknown to me, Greer came out of the room and indicated to Mary that Anne had just died. Then Mary's cell phone rang; it was Andrew. Mary told her husband the news and then simply passed the phone to me for Andrew to tell me directly about this verse. Once the brief call had ended I looked at Greer, who simply nodded a confirmation that Anne was gone. Philip and I embraced and sobbed our hearts out with gut-wrenching groans at our loss.

After a while, I went in the room and saw for myself that Anne had died. Her valiant struggle was over; she was "free at last."[3] I then picked up a Bible and shared the verse with Mary, Philip, and Greer; it came from Psalm 116:15: "*Precious in the sight of the* Lord *is the death of his faithful ones.*" It was a very profound moment for all of us.

We all had opportunities to see Anne, to weep, and to say our final farewells. But there comes an awkward moment when I, as her husband, must leave the room for the very last time. As I saw her peaceful body, I was promptly reminded of the angels' message to the visitors at the tomb on Easter morning: "Why do you look for the living among the dead?"[4] It was indeed time to go.

The funeral service was intense, but—at least from my perspective—beautiful, containing powerful music and appropriate readings. It was also evocative because of Mary's meditation, an excerpt of which is given below:

3. The first line of the old spiritual, "Free at last, free at last; I thank God I'm free at last," adapted and immortalized in Martin Luther King Jr.'s "I Have a Dream" speech, resonated strongly with me. I—and others—envisioned Anne using those words to powerfully express her newfound freedom from her diseased body.

4. Luke 24:5.

One of the most reassuring conversations concerning death recorded for us in the Bible is the one between Jesus and Martha, the sister of Lazarus (John 11:1–44). Jesus was close friends with Lazarus and his two sisters, Mary and Martha. One day, Lazarus became seriously ill. The sisters sent for Jesus to come because they believed that Jesus would be able to heal their brother. In much the same way that we, over the past few years, have often gathered together to ask God to heal Anne. Jesus, however, did not come as quickly as the sisters would have liked, and before he arrived, Lazarus died. So when Jesus arrived, Martha went out to meet him, and she was pretty upset with him. She said, "Lord, if you had been here, my brother would not have died." And *we* say, "Lord, we know you could have healed Anne, and now she's died."

Listen to how Jesus replies to Martha. I believe he is saying the same words to us here today: "I am the resurrection and the life. Those who believe in me, even though they die, will live, and everyone who lives and believes in me will never die."[5]

Martha must just have been staring at Jesus, because Jesus then asks Martha the all-important question, "*Do you believe this?*" I'll tell you one thing for sure—Anne believed this. Anne was not afraid of death—she had the absolute assurance that God loved her, and that good things awaited her after she left her sick body. She was sad to leave Tim and Philip, but never doubted that she herself was headed for eternal life, face-to-face with God. Martha believed it too. She answered Jesus, "Yes, Lord, I believe that you are the Messiah, the Son of God, the one coming into the world" (John 11:27). The question Jesus asked Martha is an eternal question, one that each one of us is free to answer in our own way.

I'm closing today by sharing with you a visual image that Tim has found helpful over the last few years, and one which was very vivid in Anne's last few days and nights in the hospital. It's an image to do with high-wire trapeze artists. Cirque de Soleil used to do a high-wire routine that was breathtakingly beautiful, but so difficult to do that only very few artists could do it. This is how it worked. There were four swings suspended from the roof, high above the floor; one swing in each corner. Gradually, the artists would make the swings go higher and higher. They would do this for quite some time—getting a rhythm going—back and forth, back and forth, higher and higher. And then, at the appointed moment in time, the ones on the swing let go of the person they were holding, and those people soared through the air, high above the crowd, passed each other in midair, and were caught by their

5. John 11:25–26.

wrists by the catcher on the diagonally opposite swing. It was hard to find artists who had enough faith in their catcher to keep their body completely still as they flew through the air. Henri Nouwen interviewed one of these trapeze artists, who explained how it works:

As a flyer I must have complete trust in my catcher. The public might think that I am the great star of the trapeze, but the real star is Joe, my catcher. He has to be there for me with split-second precision and grab me out of the air as I come to him in the long jump. . . . The secret . . . is that the flyer does nothing and the catcher does everything. When I fly to Joe, I have simply to stretch out my arms and hands and wait for him to catch me and pull me safely up. . . . A flyer must fly, and a catcher must catch, and the flyer must trust, with outstretched arms, that his catcher will be there for him.[6]

About three years ago, when it was clear that Anne's cancer had spread, Tim found this imagery helpful. Tim and Anne were on the swing, swinging together. But Tim had to be willing to let go, to allow Anne to soar towards *the* Catcher. During Anne's last days, Tim let her go, and she was soaring through the air, arms outstretched, unafraid, knowing that her Catcher was there with outstretched arms, waiting to catch her. Because Tim loved Anne, he also needed to have faith in the Catcher—he needed to know that by letting her go, he was in a sense freeing her to fly towards safety, towards freedom, to a Catcher whose love will never let her go. Both Tim and Anne had great faith in the Catcher, who now has caught Anne as she flew straight into his arms.

Walking Forward as a One-Legged Man

We had a memorial service for Anne in Manchester, England, a few weeks after she died. This was important, as most relatives were not able to come to Canada for the funeral. It was fitting to have this service in St. James' Anglican Church, Didsbury, the church where we were married and where Anne's father, Ernest, worshiped. Necessary though the service was, I was not really looking forward to the emotional intensity of another event so soon after the funeral.

Christine Sandiford, who led the service, spoke of C. S. Lewis, who published a little book (initially under a pseudonym) called *A Grief*

6. Nouwen, *Spiritual Direction*, 148–49.

Observed. This well-known work relates his many thoughts and feelings during the early months following the death of his wife, Joy Davidman, things that he had jotted down in exercise books in an effort to help him cope with his grief. Later he questioned whether he would ever get over the intense emotions and mental turmoil he was experiencing. In one section he wondered, quite bluntly, if the loss of his beloved wife was a bit like an amputation:

> To say the patient is getting over it after an operation for appendicitis is one thing; after he's had his leg off is quite another. After that operation either the wounded stump heals or the man dies. If it heals, the fierce, continuous pain will stop. Presently he'll get back his strength and be able to stump about on his wooden leg. He has "got over it." But he will probably have recurrent pains in the stump all his life, and perhaps pretty bad ones; and he will always be a one-legged man. There will be hardly any moment when he forgets it. Bathing, dressing, sitting down and getting up again, even lying in bed, will all be different. His whole way of life will be changed. . . . At present I am learning to get around on crutches. Perhaps I shall presently be given a wooden leg. But I shall never be a biped again.[7]

I miss Anne. I woke up one morning wishing I could put my arms around her, but obviously she was not there. As the old song by The Police says, "The bed's too big without you." But as I lay quietly thinking before getting up, I heard the birds chirping excitedly outside of my window. It is now early April, three months since Anne died. It is still frosty in the mornings, the grass is still brown and there are, as yet, no leaves on the trees. But the silence of the long Canadian winter is drawing to a close. Spring is coming; the birds are singing again. It is a reminder of hope and of good things still to come for this one-legged man.

A Time to Cry, a Time to Wait, a Time to Celebrate

During the first Lent after Anne died, I read an excellent little book, *Christians at the Cross*. The author, N. T. Wright, through a series of sermons, encouraged us to join in with the disciples and walk with Jesus during Easter week, beginning with Palm Sunday and heading toward Calvary where he encouraged us to lay down our burdens. After one particular chapter I was

7. Lewis, *Grief Observed*, 52–53.

shocked by my emotional reaction. I suddenly saw clearly the reality of the journey that Anne and I had traveled over the previous six years. In a sense I had been putting one foot in front of the other for a long time, but now I turned around and saw the long downhill path that we had walked together. It was an overwhelming sight and I began to cry. Anne and I had been very much aware of Jesus walking besides us on this path, but I now further recognized that Jesus had walked a similar path also knowing that it would eventually lead to *his* death.[8] Envisioning the image of that long hill, the magnitude of the journey suddenly became very vivid. Then, turning my head back to see Jesus walking beside me, it was as if I had a brief glimpse of his facial expression which simply said, "*I know*." It was a moment of recognition and acknowledgment of something in common. Jesus not only walked beside us but knew *exactly* what we experienced. Sometimes we say this all too glibly, that "God understands what it is like to be human because of Jesus Christ," but now I knew in my heart that he really did; Christ's tears and pain were real.

What did I put at the foot of the cross on that first Good Friday after Anne died? The loss of Anne and the loss of the future we might have had together. Of course I am not naive, this letting go, this grieving, is a process. But the cross is the appropriate place to bring my dashed hopes and dreams. I know the situation Anne and I faced, and the one I am now in, will be very different from your own journey. Nevertheless, we—and those we love—all face hardships. Life is not easy. Easter Week is a good time to reflect on that fact and do something positive about it as we walk with Jesus toward the cross. He knows of our disappointments and sorrows. Let us *not* hold on tight to them and so allow them to define or enslave us.

At our church that Good Friday, Mary spoke of redemption and its meaning in the context of slavery and debt—which was outlined in chapter 3. She spoke of the power in the cross of Christ to set us free. Mary went on to explain Jesus' statement, "It is finished," as "paid-in-full"—*redeemed*. However, we often live as if we were still enslaved. What are we to do? N. T. Wright says,

> [We are] *to claim in prayer that victory over the powers which Jesus won on the cross:* to hold the grief and pain of our community, and of our hearts, within the love which went to Calvary for us;

---

8. I believe Jesus was fully aware of what he was doing in going to Jerusalem. Jesus knew, as most people did, that would-be messiahs always ended up being killed by the Romans.

to pray that as the grains of wheat fall into the earth and die they will bear much fruit (John 12:24); and to work for that fruit, that new hope, that regeneration at every level, which God will give in his own time and his own way. The frustrating thing, as always, is that I don't know and you don't know how God is going to do new things here, in our own lives or our own communities. That is why we need to cling on for dear life to the story of Jesus. . . . And that is why we shall stand at the foot of the cross on Good Friday, to bring our griefs and sorrows, our bereavement and our puzzlement, to the one who has gone down into the darkness on our behalf.[9]

We enacted that symbolically by writing on pieces of paper, in complete privacy, the issues that enslave us, that limit us from experiencing the abundant life of which Jesus spoke (John 10:10). Then people were invited to place them in a fire at the foot of a huge cross at the front of the church. We then need to hang on tight to the hope within the Easter story, knowing that resurrection follows dying, as day follows night.

Easter Day is *the* day of celebration in the Christian calendar. N. T. Wright reckons that the church does not celebrate this event enough—he says we should have forty days of feasting after the forty days of fasting in Lent! We should rejoice with champagne, good food, good company, and fun-filled activities for "Jesus is risen indeed, Hallelujah!"

This idea appealed to Anne and me. Part of Anne's vision of heaven was a huge cheese and wine party, with the very best of both! So the first Easter Sunday after Anne's death, close friends who were with us during her last ten days in hospital met for an informal celebration lunch. We implicitly knew the common bond we shared and that brought us together as we had champagne, sparkling grape juice, cheese and crackers, and a special meal. The atmosphere was relaxed, chatty, and—as it should—contained laughter and joy. We toasted Anne; what better way to acknowledge that what happened to our savior on that first Easter Day is the firm expectation of what will happen to all of those who are "in Christ." As Paul reminds us in Romans 8:38–39,

> For I am convinced that neither death, nor life, nor angels, nor rulers, nor things present, nor things to come, nor powers, nor height, nor depth, nor anything else in all creation, will be able to separate us from the love of God in Christ Jesus our Lord.

---

9. Wright, *Christians at the Cross*, 28, his emphasis.

The Adventure Is Just Beginning

The question, "Where is Anne now?" is one that is privately, if not publicly, asked at every funeral. Most Christians instinctively say "heaven" or "home," as if that were the final destination. But is that the case? While Anne was alive, our Thursday book study group read N. T. Wright's *Surprised by Hope*, a book that presents a compelling biblical portrayal of the Christian hope. Jesus told the thief on the cross, "Today you will be with me in paradise" (Luke 23:43). Tom Wright explains carefully the first-century Jewish expectations of the three different terms: paradise, resurrection, and heaven; they are not synonymous.

Like the thief, Anne is now in paradise. What that means is not absolutely clear, but it is *not* heaven, so it is not her final destination, so to speak. That comes later. Heaven is "life after life after death," as N. T. Wright puts it. I do not know if Anne has any awareness of temporal sequences at the moment—not that it troubles me. Could it be like an idealized surgical anesthetic, where one moment you go "under" and the very next thing you are aware of is the Day of the Lord? Each individual would be "unconscious" for what to an outside observer would be varying lengths of time, but to the person involved just an instant? I am merely speculating, of course. I do not know. Who of us can? If, however, a sense of time still *does* have some meaning in paradise, then what Anne and others are likely experiencing is a state of bliss, peace, joy, and hope-filled refreshment while waiting for their new resurrection bodies. Moreover, we can be sure they are deeply aware of the Trinity's presence.

But what Anne is waiting for, like every one of us, is her new resurrection body (Phil 3:20–21)—the kind of body Jesus already has *now*. Like Jesus, our resurrection bodies will somehow be physical, but not in the same way as our present bodies. We will not be floating around as disembodied souls or spirits, rather we will have immortal bodies that have physical dimensions, except they will not age, decay, or get sick. Timothy Keller writes,

> Our future is not an ethereal, impersonal form of consciousness. We will not float through the air, but rather eat, embrace, sing, laugh, and dance in the kingdom of God, in degrees of power, glory and joy that we can't at present imagine.[10]

The early Christians, because of their experience with the risen Jesus, viewed the resurrection body not as an immaterial spirit, but a body in the sense of

10. Keller, *Prodigal God*, 116–17.

a physical object occupying space and time. It will be a *transformed* body, a body whose material, created from old material, will have new properties. Consequently, the contrast is not between what we call physical and nonphysical (or spirit) but between *corruptible physicality* and *incorruptible physicality*. N. T. Wright explains,

> [Our] new body will be immortal. That is, it will have passed *beyond* death not just in the *temporal* sense (that it happens to have gone through a particular moment and event) but also in the *ontological* sense of no longer being subject to sickness, injury, decay, and death itself. None of these destructive forces will have any power over the new body. That indeed may be one of the ways of understanding the *strangeness* of the risen body of Jesus. The disciples were looking at the first, and so far only, piece of incorruptible physicality.[11]

It is not just that we will have new resurrection bodies, God will restore the whole of creation as well. God's good creation—physicality—is to be rescued! We have no comprehension of the physics, chemistry, and biology of this redeemed creation; nevertheless, this was the expectation of the biblical authors. In Revelation, John the Seer writes,

> Then I saw a new heaven and a new earth; the first heaven and the first earth had passed away, and the sea was no more. . . . And I heard a loud voice from the throne saying: "See, the home of God is among mortals. He will dwell with them; they will be his peoples, and God himself will be with them; he will wipe every tear from their eyes. Death will be no more; mourning and crying and pain will be no more, for the first things have passed away." And the one who was seated on the throne said, "See I am making all things new." Also he said, "Write this, for these words are trustworthy and true."[12]

Finally, the long "exile" is over and *all* things will be put to right. Evil will be defeated and banished forever. John's majestic vision uses imagery from the Old Testament prophets, like Isaiah:

> Everlasting joy shall be upon their heads; they shall obtain joy and gladness, and sorrow and sighing shall flee away.[13]

---

11. Wright, *Surprised by Hope*, 160, his emphasis.
12. Rev 21:1, 3–5.
13. Isa 35:10.

I am about to create new heavens and a new earth; the former things shall not be remembered or come to mind. But be glad and rejoice forever in what I am creating . . . no more shall the sound of weeping be heard in it, or the cry of distress.[14]

These are wonderful words of comfort and hope, especially pertinent at a time of bereavement. On the first Easter Sunday, God gave us a glimpse of the future in the present through the bodily resurrection of Jesus the Messiah. This is what Christians *celebrate* on Easter Sunday! Anne's life is far from being over; her adventure has just begun!

14. Isa 65:17, 18a, 19b.

"Of course, Daughter of Eve," said the Faun. "The further up and the further in you go, the bigger everything gets. The inside is larger than the outside." . . .

Then Aslan turned to them and said: "You do not yet look happy as I meant you to be."

Lucy said, "We're so afraid of being sent away, Aslan. And you have sent us back into our own world so often."

"No fear of that," said Aslan. "Have you not guessed? . . . All of you are—as you used to call it in the Shadowlands—dead. The term is over; the holidays have begun. The dream is ended: this is the morning."

And as He spoke He no longer looked to them like a lion; but the things that began to happen after were so great and beautiful that I cannot write them. And for us this is the end of all the stories, and we can most truly say that they all lived happily ever after. But for them it was only the beginning of the real story. All their life in the world and all their adventures in Narnia had only been the cover and title-page: now at last they were beginning Chapter One of the Great Story which no one on earth has read: which goes on forever: in which every chapter is better than the one before.[1]

1. Lewis, *Last Battle*, 207, 210–11.

Appendix

Is Satan *Real?*

The issue of the (ontological) reality of a personal devil is an important issue to numerous Christians. Many would claim that to even suggest that Satan does not exist as some kind of demonic being is not only unbiblical, but downplays the seriousness of evil and sin. Moreover, the New Testament speaks of spiritual warfare (e.g., Eph 6:10–17; 1 Pet 5:8–10), implying that evil has intentionality and purpose—namely, to impede and frustrate the reign of God—and we typically associate such attributes with personhood. It is a legitimate concern. Those pastors, churches, and chaplains at the cutting edge of kingdom of God activities know from experience that God's reign does not advance effortlessly into a vacuum but faces energy-sapping distractions, disunity, and disorder. Such resistance tends to undermine God's mission (*missio Dei*) within a local community and the wider world. Evidently, and sadly, it often succeeds—as the New Testament writers also knew. Yet many theologians don't (or won't) speak openly of an oppositional satanic figurehead, preferring instead to demythologize demons. This is not necessarily misguided thinking; much depends on the individual's motivation. After all, if you take the *d* out of "devil" you still end up with a four-letter word! But all this makes one wonder if there is not a discontinuity between theologians in their ivory towers and ministers at the coalface. If so, there is a serious mismatch between "theory" (theology) and "practice" (praxis), one which damages God's church and mission.

There are those who argue that evil is the *absence* of the good. This is not a modern idea, but one that has a long history in Christian thought.[2] Thomas Aquinas, following St. Augustine, wrote:

2. In fact it was absorbed from Neoplatonism through the influence of people like Plotinus (ca. 205–270) on St. Augustine.

> Evil is *nothing else* than a privation of that which a thing is natu-
> rally apt to have and ought to have. But a privation is not an es-
> sence, but a negation in a substance.[3]

Just like true black absorbs all light and reflects nothing, and therefore
is not a color in itself, so we cannot appreciate goodness without contrast-
ing it with the lack thereof. (This might imply evil is an illusion, which
I reject.) Alternatively, consider the following: there is no such thing as
a "bad apple" in itself, just varieties of good apples (honey crisp, granny
smiths, gala, cox's, etc.) that have lost some of their goodness.[4] In this way
evil is seen as a malfunction of something within God's good creation. Evil
as nonbeing, then, means evil is not something that exists in itself, rather
evil is real in the sense that it is *experienced*. This important distinction can
be extended to Satan; contesting the devil's personhood does not deny the
experiential reality of evil.

Walter Wink prefers to think of the "powers" (to use Paul's term in
Rom 8:38–39) as impersonal entities, although he freely admits there is no
sure way to settle the question.[5] He cautions against our natural tendency
to automatically personalize anything that seems to act intentionally. He
makes a helpful analogy: a computer virus is an example of a systemic process that is self-replicating, contagious, and behaves almost willfully even
though it is quite impersonal. Yet anyone who has lost computer files to a
virus knows how *personal* this feels![6] Consequently, Wink wants to focus
on our experience of the powers and not be distracted by their actual (ontological) status.

In addition to personal slavery to powers (like alcohol, drugs, pornog-
raphy, phobias, and ambition)[7] there are larger, systemic evils (like racism,
sexism, classism, and consumerism) and other evils (like genocide) that
are fueled by ideologies. Capitalism enables the rich to get richer at the
expense of the poor, who are held in bondage and oppression so that the

---

3. Aquinas, *Summa Theologica*, bk. 3, ch. 7, 343, emphasis mine. Nevertheless, he still believed in angels!

4. Rice, *Search for Meaning*, 53.

5. Wink, *Powers That Be*, 27.

6. Even so, a computer virus does not arise randomly but intentionally by a program-mer. Temptation also feels *personal* (and hence targeted) else it is not an effective or genuine temptation.

7. One must add to that list the love of affluence, influence, and pleasure. If such things are our prime motivators—whether consciously or subconsciously—then they become encaptivating, *idolatrous*, powers.

wealthy can maintain their comfort. This happens at an individual level, as well as within commercial and financial businesses in a global economy, and between nation states. Walter Wink makes the important association between unseen, but undoubtedly real, spiritual powers and social institutions, companies, and other larger networks.[8] The "angel" of the corporate identity is not simply the sum total of all it is, but also bears the message of what it ought to be.[9] If, however, such powers are based on—or tainted by—idolatrous values, one ends up with an entire system of "domination." These impersonal spiritual realities are at the center of institutional life and are a force to be reckoned with—as anyone who has tried to alter a company's or institution's ethos will know. Wink concludes,

> Evil is not just personal, but structural and spiritual. It is not simply the result of human actions, but the consequence of huge systems over which no individual has full control. Only by confronting the spirituality of an institution *and* its physical manifestations can the total structure be transformed. Any attempt to transform a social system without addressing both its spirituality and its outer forms is doomed to failure. Materialism knows nothing of an inner dimension and so is blind to its effects.[10]

Astute and important though this undoubtedly is, I still think there are situations where you can imagine that evil is not only more than the sum of its parts, but has a life of its own. Consider gang rape, dog fighting, rioting, looting, or hooliganism (say, at sports venues or rallies). The communal aspect of these actions results in them taking on a vitality or identity of their own. There is a sense that these violent and depraved actions, incited by ringleaders, multiply as they feed on themselves. Some individuals may later regret their actions, ones they would never have contemplated had they been on their own. Such is the insidious power of peer pressure. There are other malicious actions by individuals, such as torture, child abuse, and rape—especially baby rape, that are (or should be) so abhorrent and *inhuman* that the notion of evil's real existence becomes credible. Add to that the horrors of the Holocaust and, alas, more recent mass genocides and other brutal war crimes, and assigning a real existence to evil becomes quite believable. One can be sympathetic with those who want to give such

8. This can be extended to departments, educational establishments, hospitals, etc., and to *churches!*

9. Ibid., 30.

10. Ibid., 31.

an existence a *mind*, so as to reflect evil's intentionality. But it does not follow that evil should be ascribed *individuality*, let alone those stereotypical portrayals of demons and Satan.[11] Nevertheless, this description portrays evil as *active* rather than merely a passive absence of the good.

Late in life (in 1960), C. S. Lewis wrote a postscript to his famed *Screwtape Letters*, first published in 1941 (and dedicated to J. R. R. Tolkien). In response to the question commonly asked of him, "Do you believe in demons?" he writes,

> I do. That is to say. I believe in angels and I believe that some of these, by the abuse of their free will, have become enemies to God and, as a corollary, to us. These we may call devils. . . . I believe this not in the sense that it is part of my creed, but in the sense that it is one of my opinions. My religion would not be in ruins if this opinion were shown to be false. Till that happens—and proofs of a negative are hard to come by—I shall retain it. It seems to me to explain a good many facts. It agrees with the plain sense of Scripture, the tradition of Christendom, and the beliefs of most men at most times. And it conflicts with nothing that any of the sciences has shown to be true.[12]

More recently, N. T. Wright has given a helpful summary concerning "the satan" (Hebrew: *ha satan*, or "the accuser"). It is worth relating his view at length:

> Evil has a hidden dimension; there is more to it than meets the eye. This extra element, I believe, includes a force or forces which are no less real for being difficult to describe. . . . The biblical picture of the satan is thus of a nonhuman and nondivine quasi-personal force which seems bent on attacking and destroying creation in general and humankind in particular, and above all on thwarting God's project of remaking the world and human beings in and through Jesus Christ and the Holy Spirit. . . . It is wrong to think of the satan as "personal" in the same way that God or Jesus is "personal"—which is not to say that the satan is a vague or nebulous force. Quite the reverse: I prefer to use the term "subpersonal" or

11. What the Bible has to say about angels, demons, and Satan is limited. Precisely because of our limited knowledge of other created agents, like angels, we do not know what responsibilities, roles, and limitations they have in the physical and spiritual realms. It would appear that, at the very least, angels can act as God's messengers.

12. Lewis, *Screwtape Letters*, 230–31. Lewis also pointed out the danger of two opposite extremes concerning Satan, who would be most happy with either; one is the denial that Satan exists and the other is to give him too much credit; ibid., xi.

"quasi-personal" as a way of refusing to accord the satan the full dignity of personhood while recognizing that the concentration of activity (its subtle schemes and devices) can and does strike us as very much like that which we associate with personhood. There are undoubtedly foolish and unhelpful ways of portraying the satan, not least in the popular imagination, and we are right to avoid them. But we shouldn't think that by doing so we have eliminated the reality to which these trivializing images point.[13]

Wink and Wright articulate their nuanced views of evil with clarity and, I think, exhibit profound insight. And both recognize evil's sinister power to enslave and blind us—and from which we need rescuing. C. S. Lewis would totally agree. However we ultimately regard *ha satan*, we should join with the Old Testament prophets and exhibit righteous anger toward evil and all its insidious effects. And then, empowered by the Spirit, do something positive to alleviate suffering in God's good—but untamed—world.

13. Wright, *Evil and the Justice of God*, 107–9, 111–12.

Bibliography

Andrew, Brother, et al. *God's Smuggler*. Expanded ed. Bloomington, MN: Chosen, 2015.

Aquinas, Thomas. *Summa Theologica*. Translated by Fathers of the English Dominican Province. 3 vols. New York: Benziger, 1947. http://www.ccel.org/ccel/aquinas/summa.

Aulén, Gustaf. *Christus Victor: An Historical Study of the Three Main Types of the Idea of Atonement*. Translated by A. G. Herbert. American ed. New York: Macmillan, 1951.

Barbour, Ian G. *Religion and Science: Historical and Contemporary Issues*. New York: HarperCollins, 1997.

Beilby, James K., and Paul R. Eddy, eds. *The Nature of Atonement: Four Views*. Downers Grove: IVP Academic, 2006.

Birch, Bruce C., et al. *A Theological Introduction to the Old Testament*. 2nd ed. Nashville: Abingdon, 2005.

Boring, M. Eugene. "Matthew." In vol. 8 of *The New Interpreter's Bible*, edited by Leander E. Keck. Nashville: Abingdon, 1994.

Boyd, Gregory A. *God at War: The Bible and Spiritual Conflict*. Downers Grove: InterVarsity, 1997.

———. *God of the Possible: A Biblical Introduction to Open Theism*. Grand Rapids: Baker, 2000.

———. *Is God to Blame? Beyond Pat Answers to the Problem of Suffering*. Downers Grove: InterVarsity, 2003.

———. *Satan and the Problem of Evil: Constructing a Trinitarian Warfare Theodicy*. Downers Grove: InterVarsity, 2001.

Bray, Gerald, ed. *Romans*. Ancient Christian Commentary on Scripture: New Testament 6. Downers Grove: InterVarsity, 1998.

Brown, Colin. *Miracles and the Critical Mind*. 1984. Reprint, Pasadena, CA: Fuller Seminary Press, 2006.

Bruce, F. F. *Tyndale New Testament Commentaries: Romans*. Downers Grove: InterVarsity, 1985.

Calvin, John. *Commentaries on the Epistle of Paul the Apostle to the Romans*. Translated and edited by John Owen. http://www.ccel.org/ccel/calvin/calcom38.html.

———. *Institutes of the Christian Religion*. Translated by Henry Beveridge. http://www.ccel.org/ccel/calvin/institutes.html.

Chadwick, Henry. *The Early Church*. Rev. ed. Penguin History of the Church 1. London: Penguin, 1993.

Cobb, John B., Jr., and Clark H. Pinnock, eds. *Searching for an Adequate God: A Dialogue between Process and Free Will Theists*. Grand Rapids: Eerdmans, 2000.

Conrad, E. W. "Satan." In *New Interpreter's Dictionary of the Bible*, 5:112–16. Nashville: Abingdon, 2009.

Davis, Stephen T., ed. *Encountering Evil: Live Options in Theodicy*. 2nd ed. Louisville: Westminster John Knox, 2001.

Downing, David C. *The Most Reluctant Convert: C. S. Lewis's Journey to Faith*. Downers Grove: InterVarsity, 2002.

Dunn, James D. G. "2 Timothy." In vol. 11 of *The New Interpreter's Bible*, edited by Leander E. Keck. Nashville: Abingdon, 2000.

Ehrman, Bart D. *God's Problem: How the Bible Fails to Answer Our Most Important Question—Why We Suffer*. New York: HarperOne, 2008.

Enns, Peter. *The Bible Tells Me So: Why Defending Scripture Has Made Us Unable to Read It*. New York: HarperOne, 2014.

———. *The Evolution of Adam: What the Bible Does and Doesn't Say about Human Origins*. Grand Rapids: Brazos, 2012.

Evans, C. Stephen, and R. Zachary Manis. *Philosophy of Religion: Thinking about Faith*. 2nd ed. Downers Grove: InterVarsity, 2009.

Fergusson, David. *Creation*. Guides to Theology. Grand Rapids: Eerdmans, 2014.

Fitzmyer, Joseph A. *Romans: A New Translation with Introduction and Commentary*. Anchor Bible 33. New York: Doubleday, 1993.

Frankl, Viktor E. *Man's Search for Meaning: An Introduction to Logotherapy*. Translated by Ilse Lasch. London: Hodder and Stoughton, 1964.

Fretheim, Terence E. *Creation Untamed: The Bible, God, and Natural Disasters*. Grand Rapids: Baker, 2010.

———. *God and World in the Old Testament: A Relational Theology of Creation*. Nashville: Abingdon, 2005.

———. *The Suffering of God: An Old Testament Perspective*. Philadelphia: Fortress, 1984.

Griffin, David Ray. "Creation out of Nothing, Creation out of Chaos, and the Problem of Evil." In *Encountering Evil: Live Options in Theodicy*, edited by Stephen T. Davis, 108–25, 137–44 [Rejoinder]. 2nd ed. Louisville: Westminster John Knox, 2001.

Gunton, Colin E. *The Triune Creator: A Historical and Systematic Study*. Grand Rapids: Eerdmans, 1998.

Hall, Douglas John. *The Cross in Our Context*. Minneapolis: Fortress, 2003.

———. *The End of Christendom and the Future of Christianity*. Eugene, OR: Wipf & Stock, 2002.

———. *God and Human Suffering: An Exercise in the Theology of the Cross*. Minneapolis: Augsburg, 1986.

Hasker, William. *The Triumph of God over Evil: Theodicy for a World of Suffering*. Downers Grove: InterVarsity, 2008.

Hauerwas, Stanley, and William H. Willimon. *The Holy Spirit*. Nashville: Abingdon, 2015.

Heim, S. Mark. *Saved from Sacrifice: A Theology of the Cross*. Grand Rapids: Eerdmans, 2006.

Holtzen, Wm. Curtis, and Roberto Sirvent, eds. *By Faith and Reason: The Essential Keith Ward*. London: Darton, Longman & Todd, 2012.

Hunter, Ian, ed. *The Very Best of Malcolm Muggeridge*. Vancouver: Regent College Publishing, 1998.

Jewett, Robert. *Romans: A Commentary*. Minneapolis: Fortress, 2007.

Jones, James. *Why Do People Suffer?* Peabody: Henderson, 2007.

Jowers, Dennis W., ed. *Four Views on Divine Providence.* Grand Rapids: Zondervan, 2011.

Kant, Immanuel. *The Conflict of the Faculties.* Translated by Mary J. Gregor. New York: Abaris, 1979.

Keller, Timothy. *The Prodigal God.* New York: Riverhead, 2008.

———. *The Reason for God: Belief in an Age of Skepticism.* New York: Dutton, 2008.

———. *Walking with God through Pain and Suffering.* New York: Dutton, 2013.

Kushner, Harold S. *When Bad Things Happen to Good People.* New York: Schocken, 1981.

Leupp, Roderick T. *Knowing the Name of God: A Trinitarian Tapestry of Grace, Faith and Community.* Downers Grove: InterVarsity, 1996.

Levenson, Jon D. *Creation and the Persistence of Evil: The Jewish Drama of Divine Omnipotence.* Princeton: Princeton University Press, 1988.

Lewis, C. S. *A Grief Observed.* New York: HarperOne, 1961.

———. *The Last Battle.* New York: HarperCollins, 1956.

———. *Mere Christianity.* New York: HarperCollins, 2001.

———. *Miracles: A Preliminary Study.* New York: HarperCollins, 2001.

———. *The Screwtape Letters.* New York: HarperCollins, 1961.

Long, Thomas G. *What Shall We Say? Evil, Suffering, and the Crisis of Faith.* Grand Rapids: Eerdmans, 2011.

McGrath, Alister E. *Christian Theology: An Introduction.* 5th ed. Chichester: Wiley-Blackwell, 2011.

Migliore, Daniel L. *Faith Seeking Understanding: An Introduction to Christian Theology.* 2nd ed. Grand Rapids: Eerdmans, 2004.

Moltmann, Jürgen. *Collected Readings.* Edited by Margaret Kohl. Minneapolis: Fortress, 2014.

Newbigin, Lesslie. *Proper Confidence: Faith, Doubt, and Certainty in Christian Discipleship.* Grand Rapids: Eerdmans, 1995.

Noll, Mark A. *Turing Points: Decisive Moments in the History of Christianity.* 3rd ed. Grand Rapids: Baker, 2012.

Nouwen, Henri. *Spiritual Direction.* New York: HarperCollins, 2006.

Olson, Roger E. *Against Calvinism.* Grand Rapids: Zondervan, 2011.

Oord, Thomas Jay. *The Uncontrolling Love of God: An Open and Relational Account of Providence.* Downers Grove: IVP Academic, 2015.

Park, Andrew Sung. *Triune Atonement: Christ's Healing for Sinners, Victims, and the Whole Creation.* Louisville: Westminster John Knox, 2009.

Peacocke, Arthur. *Theology for a Scientific Age: Being and Becoming—Natural, Divine and Human.* Minneapolis: Fortress, 1993.

Peterson, Michael, et al. *Reason and Religious Belief: An Introduction to the Philosophy of Religion.* 4th ed. Oxford: Oxford University Press, 2009.

Pinnock, Clark H. *Most Moved Mover: A Theology of God's Openness.* Grand Rapids: Baker, 2001.

Plantinga, Alvin. *God, Evil, and Freedom.* Grand Rapids: Eerdmans, 1974.

Plantinga, Richard J., et al. *An Introduction to Christian Theology.* Cambridge: Cambridge University Press, 2010.

Polkinghorne, John. *Exploring Reality: The Intertwining of Science and Religion.* New Haven: Yale University Press, 2005.

———. *The Faith of a Physicist.* Minneapolis: Fortress, 1996.

———. "Kenotic Creation and Divine Action." In *The Work of Love: Creation as Kenosis*, edited by John Polkinghorne, 90–106. Grand Rapids: Eerdmans, 2001.

———. *Reason and Reality: The Relationship between Science and Theology*. London: SPCK, 1991.

———. *Science and Creation: The Search for Understanding*. London: SPCK, 1988.

———. *Science and Providence: God's Interaction with the World*. West Conshohocken, PA: Templeton Foundation, 2005.

———. *Testing Scripture: A Scientist Explores the Bible*. Grand Rapids: Brazos, 2010.

———, ed. *The Work of Love: Creation as Kenosis*. Grand Rapids: Eerdmans, 2001.

Pullinger, Jackie, and Andrew Quicke. *Chasing the Dragon*. Rev. ed. Bloomington, MN: Chosen, 2001.

Rahner, Karl. *The Trinity*. Translated by Joseph Donceel. New York: Herder and Herder, 1970.

Reddish, Tim. *Science and Christianity: Foundations and Frameworks for Moving Forward in Faith*. Eugene, OR: Wipf & Stock, 2016.

Rice, Richard. *Suffering and the Search for Meaning: Contemporary Responses to the Problem of Pain*. Downers Grove: InterVarsity, 2014.

Rohr, Richard. *The Divine Dance: The Trinity and Your Transformation*. With Mike Morrell. London: SPCK, 2016.

———. *Job and the Mystery of Suffering: Spiritual Reflections*. New York: Crossroad, 2015.

Rutledge, Fleming. *The Crucifixion: Understanding the Death of Jesus Christ*. Grand Rapids: Eerdmans, 2015.

Sampley, J. Paul. "1 Corinthians." In vol. 10 of *The New Interpreter's Bible*, edited by Leander E. Keck. Nashville: Abingdon, 2002.

Sanders, John, ed. *Atonement and Violence: A Theological Conversation*. Nashville: Abingdon, 2006.

———. *The God Who Risks: A Theology of Divine Providence*. 2nd ed. Downers Grove: InterVarsity, 2007.

Southgate, Christopher. *The Groaning of Creation: God, Evolution, and the Problem of Evil*. Louisville: Westminster John Knox, 2008.

Sproul, R. C. *Not a Chance: The Myth of Chance in Modern Science and Cosmology*. Grand Rapids: Baker, 1994.

Tada, Joni Eareckson. *Joni: An Unforgettable Story*. 25th anniv. ed. Grand Rapids: Zondervan, 2001.

Tada, Joni Eareckson, and Steven Estes. *When God Weeps: Why Our Sufferings Matter to the Almighty*. Grand Rapids: Zondervan, 1997.

Thiselton, Anthony C. *Systematic Theology*. London: SPCK, 2015.

Tiessen, Terrance. *Providence and Prayer: How Does God Work in the World?* Downers Grove: InterVarsity, 2000.

Walton, John H. *The Lost World of Genesis One: Ancient Cosmology and the Origins Debate*. Downers Grove: InterVarsity, 2009.

Ward, Keith. *Divine Action: Examining God's Role in an Open and Emergent Universe*. West Conshohocken, PA: Templeton Foundation, 2007.

Warren, Rick. *The Purpose Driven Life*. Grand Rapids: Zondervan, 2002.

Weaver, J. Denny. *The Nonviolent Atonement*. 2nd ed. Grand Rapids: Eerdmans, 2011.

Wells, Harold. *The Christic Center: Life-Giving and Liberating*. Maryknoll: Orbis, 2004.

White, Robert S. *Who Is to Blame? Disasters, Nature, and Acts of God*. Oxford: Monarch, 2014.

Wilkerson, David, et al. *The Cross and the Switchblade*. New York: Jove, 1977.

Wilkinson, David. *When I Pray, What Does God Do?* Oxford: Monarch, 2015.

Wink, Walter. *The Powers That Be: Theology for a New Millennium*. New York: Doubleday, 1998.

Wolterstorff, Nicholas. *Lament for a Son*. Grand Rapids: Eerdmans, 1987.

Wright, N. T. *The Challenge of Jesus: Rediscovering Who Jesus Was and Is*. Downers Grove: InterVarsity, 1999.

—————. *Christians at the Cross*. Ijamsville, MD: Word Among Us Press, 2007.

—————. *The Day the Revolution Began: Reconsidering the Meaning of Jesus's Crucifixion*. New York: HarperOne, 2016.

—————. *Evil and the Justice of God*. Downers Grove: InterVarsity, 2006.

—————. *Jesus and the Victory of God*. Minneapolis: Fortress, 1996.

—————. "The Letter to the Romans." In vol. 10 of *The New Interpreter's Bible*, edited by Leander E. Keck. Nashville: Abingdon, 2002.

—————. *Simply Jesus: A New Vision of Who He Was, What He Did, and Why He Matters*. New York: HarperOne, 2011.

—————. *Surprised by Hope: Rethinking Heaven, the Resurrection, and the Mission of the Church*. New York: HarperOne, 2008.

Yancey, Philip. *Disappointment with God*. Grand Rapids: Zondervan, 1988.

—————. *Where Is God When It Hurts?* Grand Rapids: Zondervan, 1977.

Zacharias, Ravi, and Vince Vitale. *Why Suffering? Finding Meaning and Comfort When Life Doesn't Make Sense*. New York: Faith Words, 2014.

Other Books by Tim Reddish

Science and Christianity:
Foundations and Frameworks for
Moving Forward in Faith

WIPF &
STOCK

"The polarized positions, from within the church and from skeptics outside, are so loud and so effectively disseminated that it is often difficult for sensible, mediating positions to be heard. But I am encouraged that there are more and more such positions, including this straightforward defense of critical realism. Reddish's concluding challenge to '*Let Scripture be*' should be a helpful word in season for church audiences."

—Mark Noll, Francis A. McAnaney Professor of History at the University
of Notre Dame, and author of *Jesus Christ and the Life of the Mind*

"A good book on science and faith needs to be written by someone who has a feel for science from the experience of working it, combined with a depth of theological understanding, and the lightness of touch to make it readable and exciting. Tim Reddish has written this kind of good book."

—David Wilkinson, FRAS, Principal of St. John's College, Durham, UK,
and author of *When I Pray, What Does God Do?*

"Reddish engages Scripture faithfully and science with professional integrity. In this book readers will find a helpful guide to understanding not just the perennial flash points of science and Christianity, but the deeper issues that have conditioned the modern mind to be suspicious of finding common ground between them. Reddish shows not just that science and faith can get along, but that when each is understood properly, they enrich each other."

—Jim Stump, Senior Editor, *BioLogos*,
and author of *Science and Christianity: An Introduction to the Issues*

"This is an informative book of real scholarship in which Tim Reddish addresses the supposed 'conflict' between science and Christianity head-on. By exposing the historical and cultural roots of the divide, he is able to point out where useful dialogue can and should occur."

—Bill McConkey, O. Ont, FRSC, Professor Emeritus,
University of Windsor

"In *Science and Christianity*, Tim Reddish lays an authoritative, yet personal, account of why science and Christianity are not contradictory 'belief systems.' He tackles the big questions that are routinely asked about their relationship—the nature of truth, prayer, the Bible, design in nature, miracles—and offers direct, engaging explanations that will appeal. A great book to read yourself and then give to others."

—Mike Hulme, Professor of Climate and Culture, King's College London

The Amish Farmer Who Hated L.A.:
And 8 Other Modern-day Allegories

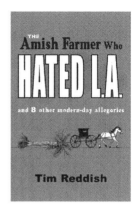

"In this book the delights of imagination meet timeless stories of Scripture. The outcome is the retelling of deep truths about both the human condition and God's remarkable grace. Tim Reddish has given us a whimsical and thought-provoking read that is also pure pleasure."

—Rev. Dr. Judy Paulsen, Professor of Evangelism,
Wycliffe College, Toronto

"Tim Reddish writes to address difficult questions from interesting angles. His work feels fresh, contemporary, challenging, and thought-provoking— without departing from orthodox faith. This book helps us to reflect on our lives, the better to serve the One who gave us life."

—Ven. Nick Barker, Archdeacon of Auckland and Priest-in-Charge of
Holy Trinity, Darlington, UK

"This collection of short stories warms the heart and provides insight into how God is at work through people today. The stories take biblical topics and situate them into contemporary cultural settings, and so help to open our eyes to their meaning for today. Tim Reddish takes on a number of interesting topics and handles them with grace."

—Dr. John Sanders, Professor of Religious Studies, Hendrix College,
and author of *The God Who Risks*

"In reading each of Tim's stories I had an '*Aha!*' moment when I realized which familiar Bible story he was depicting, only to discover an unexpected twist around the next corner. These stories are full of gentle humor and great insight which will keep the reader thinking for days after reading them."

—Rev. Dr. Stuart Macdonald, Professor of Church and Society, Knox College, Toronto

Made in the USA
Monee, IL
21 February 2020